REFLECT¹

LISTENING & SPEAKING

CYNTHIA FETTIG

D1568615

Australia · Brazil · Mexico · Singapore · United Kingdom · United States

National Geographic Learning,
a Cengage Company

Reflect 1 Listening & Speaking
Author: Cynthia Fettig

Publisher: Sherrise Roehr
Executive Editor: Laura Le Dréan
Development Editor: Lisl Bove
Director of Global Marketing: Ian Martin
Product Marketing Manager: Tracy Baillie
Senior Content Project Manager: Mark Rzeszutek
Media Researcher: Stephanie Eenigenburg
Art Director: Brenda Carmichael
Senior Designer: Lisa Trager
Operations Coordinator: Hayley Chwazik-Gee
Manufacturing Buyer: Mary Beth Hennebury
Composition: MPS Limited

For permission to use material from this text or product, submit all requests online at **cengage.com/permissions** Further permissions questions can be emailed to **permissionrequest@cengage.com**

Student Book ISBN: 978-0-357-44911-0
Student Book with Online Practice: 978-0-357-44917-2

National Geographic Learning
200 Pier 4 Boulevard
Boston, MA 02210

Locate your local office at **international.cengage.com/region**

Visit National Geographic Learning online at **ELTNGL.com**
Visit our corporate website at **www.cengage.com**

Printed in China
Print Number: 01   Print Year: 2021

SCOPE AND SEQUENCE

SPEAKING & PRONUNCIATION	GRAMMAR	CRITICAL THINKING	REFLECT ACTIVITIES
Speak with confidence Consonants and voicing	Simple present of *be* Adjectives	Personalize	▶ Introduce yourself ▶ Find things in common ▶ Discuss stereotypes ▶ **UNIT TASK** Say who you are and who you are not
Introduce a topic Vowels	Simple present Simple present negative	Categorize information	▶ Explore reasons people move ▶ Ask about activities people do at home ▶ Think about what makes a house a home ▶ **UNIT TASK** Describe what home means to you
Give reasons Syllables	Adverbs of frequency Prepositions of time	Make comparisons	▶ Compare daily activities ▶ Analyze your free time ▶ Evaluate your habits ▶ **UNIT TASK** Give a talk about a habit you want to change
Use questions Word stress	Infinitives and gerunds Sentences with *when*	Make inferences	▶ Compare eating habits ▶ Explore how food connects you to others ▶ Define what a comfort food is ▶ **UNIT TASK** Describe your comfort food

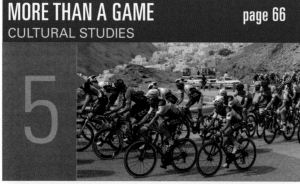

SPEAKING & PRONUNCIATION	GRAMMAR	CRITICAL THINKING	REFLECT ACTIVITIES
Use listing words and phrases Sentence Stress: Content words	Gerunds Conjunctions *and* and *but*	Brainstorm	▶ Categorize sports ▶ Explore opinions about sports ▶ Discuss uncommon sports ▶ **UNIT TASK** Debate if an activity is a sport or not
Check understanding Reduced structure words	*Be going to* Imperatives	Analyze information	▶ Analyze your entertainment preferences ▶ Discuss connecting to others online ▶ Compare activities you do alone and with others ▶ **UNIT TASK** Give a demonstration
Describe with details Connected speech	*Would like* Present continuous	Ask questions	▶ Discuss jobs ▶ Discuss what's important at work ▶ Identify skills you have ▶ **UNIT TASK** Describe your dream job
Close a presentation The focus word	Simple past of *be* Simple past	Understand metaphors	▶ Discuss environmental problems ▶ Analyze ways you help the environment ▶ Discuss your experience with climate change ▶ **UNIT TASK** Give a presentation about an important person

CONNECT TO IDEAS

Reflect Listening & Speaking features relevant, global content to engage students while helping them acquire the academic language and skills they need. Specially-designed activities give students the opportunity to reflect on and connect ideas and language to their academic, work, and personal lives.

National Geographic photography and content invite students to investigate the world and discuss high-interest topics.

Watch & Speak and **Listen & Speak** sections center on high-interest video and audio that students will want to talk about as they build academic listening and speaking skills.

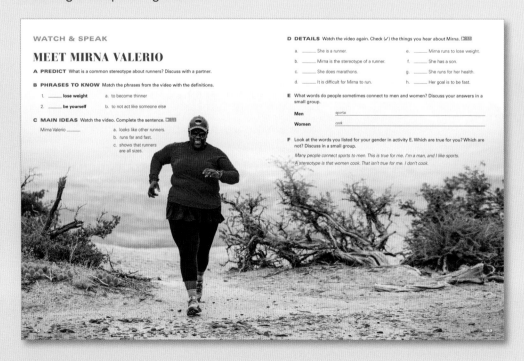

CONNECT TO ACADEMIC SKILLS

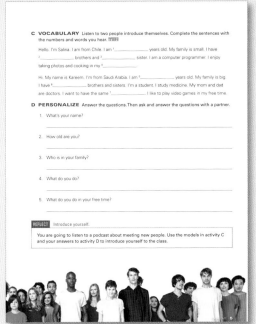

C VOCABULARY Listen to two people introduce themselves. Complete the sentences with the numbers and words you hear. [audio]

Hello. I'm Salina. I am from Chile. I am 1_____ years old. My family is small. I have 2_____ brothers and 3_____ sister. I am a computer programmer. I enjoy taking photos and cooking in my 4_____.

Hi. My name is Kareem. I'm from Saudi Arabia. I am 5_____ years old. My family is big. I have 6_____ brothers and sisters. I'm a student. I study medicine. My mom and dad are doctors. I want to have the same 7_____. I like to play video games in my free time.

D PERSONALIZE Answer the questions. Then ask and answer the questions with a partner.

1. What's your name?
2. How old are you?
3. Who is in your family?
4. What do you do?
5. What do you do in your free time?

REFLECT Introduce yourself.

You are going to listen to a podcast about meeting new people. Use the models in activity C and your answers to activity D to introduce yourself to the class.

Reflect activities give students the opportunity to think critically about what they are learning and check their understanding.

Scaffolded activities build confidence and provide students with a clear path to achieving final outcomes.

K GRAMMAR Think of three adjectives to describe a classmate. Write them down. Then tell the class. Ask your classmates to guess who you're talking about.

This person is tall. She has black hair. She is funny. Who is she?

L PLAN Choose five categories. Write an *I am* statement for three categories. Write an *I am not* statement for two categories.

Age	
Country	
Free time	
Good at	
Personality	
Not good at	
Family	
Job	
School	

SPEAKING SKILL   Speak with confidence

When you speak, it's important to speak confidently.

To speak with confidence:
▸ Practice what you plan to say.
▸ Speak loudly and clearly.
▸ Look at the audience.

M PRACTICE Use your answers in activity L to prepare your introduction. Practice introducing yourself to a partner. Practice speaking confidently.

N UNIT TASK Reintroduce yourself to the class. Say who you are and who you are not.

16 UNIT 1

Focused academic listening and speaking skills help students communicate with confidence.

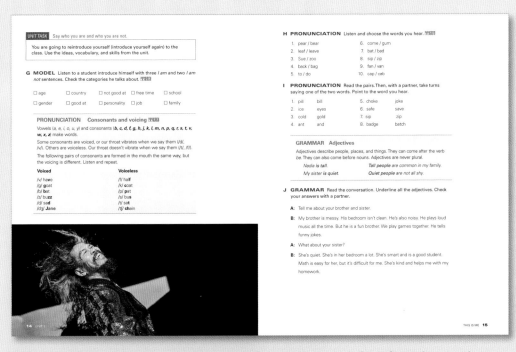

UNIT TASK Say who you are and who you are not.

You are going to reintroduce yourself (introduce yourself again) to the class. Use the ideas, vocabulary, and skills from the unit.

G MODEL Listen to a student introduce himself with three *I am* and two *I am not* sentences. Check the categories he talks about. [audio]

☐ age   ☐ country   ☐ not good at   ☐ free time   ☐ school
☐ gender   ☐ good at   ☐ personality   ☐ job   ☐ family

PRONUNCIATION   Consonants and voicing [audio]

Vowels (*a, e, i, o, u, y*) and consonants (*b, c, d, f, g, h, j, k, l, m, n, p, q, r, s, t, v, w, x, z*) make words.

Some consonants are voiced, or our throat vibrates when we say them (/d/, /v/). Others are voiceless. Our throat doesn't vibrate when we say them (/t/, /f/).

The following pairs of consonants are formed in the mouth the same way, but the voicing is different. Listen and repeat.

Voiced	**Voiceless**
/v/ have	/f/ half
/g/ goat	/k/ coat
/b/ bat	/p/ pat
/z/ buzz	/s/ bus
/d/ sad	/t/ set
/dʒ/ Jane	/tʃ/ chain

H PRONUNCIATION Listen and choose the words you hear. [audio]

1. pear / bear
2. leaf / leave
3. Sue / zoo
4. back / bag
5. to / do
6. come / gum
7. bat / bad
8. sip / zip
9. fan / van
10. cap / cab

I PRONUNCIATION Read the pairs. Then, with a partner, take turns saying one of the two words. Point to the word you hear.

1. pill   bill
2. ice   eyes
3. cold   gold
4. ant   and
5. choke   joke
6. safe   save
7. sip   zip
8. badge   batch

GRAMMAR   Adjectives

Adjectives describe people, places, and things. They can come after the verb *be*. They can also come before nouns. Adjectives are never plural.

Nadia is **tall**.   **Tall** people are common in my family.
My sister **is quiet**.   **Quiet** people are not all shy.

J GRAMMAR Read the conversation. Underline all the adjectives. Check your answers with a partner.

A: Tell me about your brother and sister.
B: My brother is messy. His bedroom isn't clean. He's also noisy. He plays loud music all the time. But he is a fun brother. We play games together. He tells funny jokes.
A: What about your sister?
B: She's quiet. She's in her bedroom a lot. She's smart and is a good student. Math is easy for her, but it's difficult for me. She's kind and helps me with my homework.

14 UNIT 1

THIS IS ME 15

Clear models, relevant grammar, and step-by-step planning give students the support they need to complete the final speaking task successfully.

CONNECT TO ACHIEVEMENT

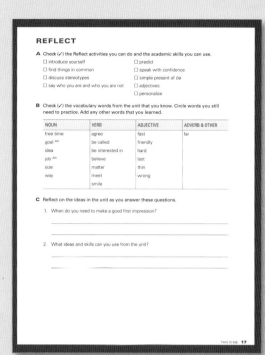

Reflect at the end of the unit is an opportunity for formative assessment. Students review the skills and vocabulary they have gained.

DIGITAL RESOURCES

TEACH lively, engaging lessons that get students speaking. The Classroom Presentation Tool helps teachers to present the Student's Book pages, play audio and video, and increase participation by providing a central focus for the class.

LEARN AND TRACK with Online Practice and Student's eBook. For students, the mobile-friendly platform optimizes learning through customized re-teaching and adaptive practice. For instructors, progress-tracking is made easy through the shared gradebook.

ASSESS learner performance and progress with the ExamView® Assessment Suite available online.

ACKNOWLEDGMENTS

The Authors and Publisher would like to acknowledge the teachers around the world who participated in the development of *Reflect*.

A special thanks to our Advisory Board for their valuable input during the development of this series.

ADVISORY BOARD

Dr. Mansoor S. Almalki, Taif University, Saudi Arabia; **John Duplice**, Sophia University, Japan; **Heba Elhadary**, Gulf University for Science and Technology, Kuwait; **Hind Elyas**, Niagara College, Saudi Arabia; **Cheryl House**, ILSC Education Group, Canada; **Xiao Luo**, BFUS International, China; **Daniel L. Paller,** Kinjo Gakuin University, Japan; **Ray Purdy**, ELS Education Services, USA; **Sarah Symes,** Cambridge Street Upper School, USA.

GLOBAL REVIEWERS

ASIA

Michael Crawford, Dokkyo University, Japan; **Ronnie Hill**, RMIT University Vietnam, Vietnam; **Aaron Nurse**, Golden Path Academics, Vietnam; **Simon Park**, Zushi Kaisei, Japan; **Aunchana Punnarungsee**, Majeo University, Thailand.

LATIN AMERICA AND THE CARIBBEAN

Leandro Aguiar, inFlux, Brazil; **Sonia Albertazzi-Osorio**, Costa Rica Institute of Technology, Costa Rica; **Auricea Bacelar**, Top Seven Idiomas, Brazil; **Natalia Benavides**, Universidad de Los Andes, Colombia; **James Bonilla**, Global Language Training UK, Colombia; **Diego Bruekers Deschamp**, Inglês Express, Brazil; **Josiane da Rosa**, Hello Idiomas, Brazil; **Marcos de Campos Bueno**, It's Cool International, Brazil; **Sophia De Carvalho**, Ingles Express, Brazil; **André Luiz dos Santos**, IFG, Brazil; **Oscar Gomez-Delgado**, Universidad de los Andes, Colombia; **Ruth Elizabeth Hibas**, Inglês Express, Brazil; **Rebecca Ashley Hibas**, Inglês Express, Brazil; **Cecibel Juliao**, UDELAS University, Panama; **Rosa Awilda López Fernández**, School of Languages UNAPEC University, Dominican Republic; **Isabella Magalhães**, Fluent English Pouso Alegre, Brazil; **Gabrielle Marchetti**, Teacher's House, Brazil; **Sabine Mary**, INTEC, Dominican Republic; **Miryam Morron**, Corporación Universitaria Americana, Colombia; **Mary Ruth Popov**, Ingles Express, Ltda., Brazil; **Leticia Rodrigues Resende**, Brazil; **Margaret Simons**, English Center, Brazil.

MIDDLE EAST

Abubaker Alhitty, University of Bahrain, Bahrain; **Jawaria Iqbal**, Saudi Arabia; **Rana Khan**, Algonquin College, Kuwait; **Mick King**, Community College of Qatar, Qatar; **Seema Jaisimha Terry**, German University of Technology, Oman.

USA AND CANADA

Thomas Becskehazy, Arizona State University, AZ; **Robert Bushong**, University of Delaware, DE; **Ashley Fifer**, Nassau Community College, NY; **Sarah Arva Grosik**, University of Pennsylvania, PA; **Carolyn Ho**, Lone Star College-CyFair, TX; **Zachary Johnsrud**, Norquest College, Canada; **Caitlin King**, IUPUI, IN; **Andrea Murau Haraway**, Global Launch / Arizona State University, AZ; **Bobbi Plante**, Manitoba Institute of Trades and Technology, Canada; **Michael Schwartz**, St. Cloud State University, MN; **Pamela Smart-Smith**, Virginia Tech, VA; **Kelly Smith**, English Language Institute, UCSD Extension, CA; **Karen Vallejo**, University of California, CA.

THIS IS ME

"Our Kind of People" is a photo project by Bayeté Ross Smith. When we look at these photos, we tell ourselves a story about this man.

CONNECT TO THE TOPIC

1. Do the man's clothes change the way he looks?

2. What do you wear at home? school? work?

PREPARE TO LISTEN

A ACTIVATE What do you say to new people? Complete the chart.

Saying hello	Questions	Saying good-bye
Hi.	How are you?	Bye.

B VOCABULARY Listen to the words. Complete the sentences with the correct form of the words. 🎧 1.1

be called (v phr)	free time (n phr)	idea (n)	meet (v)	way (n)
be interested in (v phr)	friendly (adj)	job (n)	smile (v)	wrong (adj)

1. My teacher is very _____. She says *Hello* to all the students.

2. On the first day of class, we _____ our classmates. We say our names and where we're from.

3. My brother's name is Alessandro, but at home he _____ Ale.

4. Oh, no! I'm on the _____ bus. I need a different bus.

5. I work and go to school, so I don't have a lot of _____.

6. I _____ cooking. I take a cooking class on Saturdays.

7. My family has one _____ about my future, but I have a different one.

8. Text messages are one _____ that I talk to my friends.

9. Doctors have an important _____.

10. When I'm happy, I _____.

C VOCABULARY Listen to two people introduce themselves. Complete the sentences with the numbers and words you hear.  1.2

Hello. I'm Salina. I am from Chile. I am ¹_____ years old. My family is small. I have ²_____ brothers and ³_____ sister. I am a computer programmer. I enjoy taking photos and cooking in my ⁴_____.

Hi. My name is Kareem. I'm from Saudi Arabia. I am ⁵_____ years old. My family is big. I have ⁶_____ brothers and sisters. I'm a student. I study medicine. My mom and dad are doctors. I want to have the same ⁷_____. I like to play video games in my free time.

D PERSONALIZE Answer the questions. Then ask and answer the questions with a partner.

1. What's your name?

   _____

2. How old are you?

   _____

3. Who is in your family?

   _____

4. What do you do?

   _____

5. What do you do in your free time?

   _____

REFLECT Introduce yourself.

You are going to listen to a podcast about meeting new people. Use the models in activity C and your answers to activity D to introduce yourself to the class.

FIRST IMPRESSIONS

A bridegroom meets his new
family in Rajasthan, India.

LISTENING SKILL   Predict

Before you listen, it's helpful to think about, or predict, what you might hear. To predict, look at the title, photo(s), caption(s), and any other information on the page. Then think about what you know about the topic.

A PREDICT Read the definition of *impression* and answer the questions. Then listen to the first part of the podcast and check your answers. 🎧 1.3

impression (n) a thought or idea about someone or something

1. When do we make a first impression?

   a. When we meet a new person   b. When we see our friends

2. Are there things we can do to make a good first impression?

   a. Yes   b. No

B PHRASES TO KNOW Match the phrases from the podcast with the definitions.

1. _____ **body language**   a. look at another person's eyes

2. _____ **make eye contact**   b. share the same hobbies and interests

3. _____ **have in common**   c. showing how we feel with our body

C MAIN IDEAS Listen to the podcast. Choose the three main ideas. 🎧 1.4

a. First impressions are wrong.

b. It's good to look at people's faces and clothes when you meet them.

c. Friendly people make a good first impression.

d. It's good to ask questions when you meet someone.

e. It's good to find things you have in common.

D DETAILS Listen again. Check (✓) how to make a good first impression. 🎧 1.4

- ☐ ask about age
- ☐ ask questions
- ☐ don't ask questions
- ☐ find things in comon
- ☐ go to a party
- ☐ make eye contact
- ☐ smile
- ☐ talk a lot about you
- ☐ wear nice clothes

CRITICAL THINKING   Personalize

When you personalize, you think about how something relates to your life. This helps you remember information.

E APPLY Check (✓) all the ways you meet new people. Then compare your answers with a small group. How many ways are the same?

☐ family   ☐ hobbies   ☐ online   ☐ school
☐ friends   ☐ job   ☐ neighborhood   ☐ sports
☐ other: _____

GRAMMAR   Simple present of *be*

We use *be* to describe things. Some specific uses are:

Age: *I **am** 21.*   Nationality: *The teacher **is** Australian.*

Job: *My father **is** an engineer.*   Origin: *I **am** from South Korea.*

Location: *We **are** in class.*   Time: *It **is** 9:00.*

Be has three forms in the simple present: *am*, *is*, and *are*. Add *not* to make a negative.

*I **am** a student. You **are not** the teacher. He **is** the teacher.
We **are not** from Canada.*

Subject pronouns	*Be*	Contractions
I	am (not)	I'm (not)
you/we/they	are (not)	you're/we're/they're (not)
		you/we/they aren't
he/she/it	is (not)	he's/she's/it's (not)
		he/she/it isn't

F GRAMMAR Choose the correct form of *be* to complete the text.

I like my English class. The students ¹ **isn't / aren't** from the same countries. We ² **am / are / is** from around the world. Hiro ³ **am / are / is** from Japan. Pedro and Lupita ⁴ **am / are / is** from Mexico. I ⁵ **am / are / is** from Turkey. Our teacher ⁶ **am / are / is** from Australia. I ⁷ **am / are / is** good friends with Pedro. He ⁸ **am / is / are** friendly. I ⁹ **am / are / is** interested in business. English ¹⁰ **am / are / is** good for getting a job. Pedro ¹¹ **isn't / aren't** interested in business. He ¹² **am / are / is** interested in computers. We ¹³ **isn't / aren't** in any other classes together.

G GRAMMAR Complete the sentences with the correct form of *be*. Then introduce yourself to three classmates. Follow the model.

A: Hi, my name ¹_____ Habib.

B: Hi, I ²_____ Saliah. Where ³_____ you from?

A: I ⁴_____ from the United Arab Emirates. Where ⁵_____ you from?

B: I ⁶_____ from Turkey. What do you do?

A: I ⁷_____ a student. What do you do?

B: I ⁸_____ a student, too. What do you do in your free time?

A: I enjoy reading. What do you do?

B: I play volleyball.

A: What other things ⁹_____ you interested in?

B: I ¹⁰_____ interested in languages. And you?

A: I ¹¹_____ interested in old movies.

B: It ¹²_____ nice to meet you.

A: Nice to meet you, too.

REFLECT Find things in common.

Complete the chart with information about you. Then work with a small group. Find things you have in common. Use the chart to help you. Then share what you have in common with your group.

Family	Free time	Interests	Job	Study

We all study English.
Trang and Jeremy are interested in computers.
Ahmad and I have the same job. We're both engineers.

PREPARE TO WATCH

A VOCABULARY Listen to the words. Match the words with the definitions. 🔊 1.5

1. _____ agree (v)   a. not near

2. _____ believe (v)   b. something you want to do in the future

3. _____ far (adv)   c. at the end

4. _____ fast (adj)   d. difficult

5. _____ goal (n)   e. not fat

6. _____ hard (adj)   f. how large or small something is

7. _____ last (adj)   g. quick, not slow

8. _____ matter (v)   h. to be important

9. _____ size (n)   i. to think something is true

10. _____ thin (adj)   j. to think the same as someone

B Match the words to their opposites.

1. _____ agree   a. disagree

2. _____ far   b. easy

3. _____ fast   c. fat

4. _____ hard   d. first

5. _____ last   e. near

6. _____ thin   f. slow

C PERSONALIZE Discuss the questions in a small group.

1. What **matters** a lot to you?
2. What's **hard** for you to do?
3. What is a **goal** you have?
4. Do you usually **agree** with your parents?

D Match the sayings with their meanings. Then discuss in a small group. Do you agree with them?

1. _____ Beauty comes in all **sizes**.

2. _____ Live every day like it's your **last** day.

3. _____ All things are **hard** until they're easy.

4. _____ Time flies.

a. Every day **matters**.

b. It takes time to learn things.

c. Life goes by **fast**.

d. Anyone can be beautiful.

REFLECT Discuss stereotypes.

Look at the infographic and answer the questions. Then discuss your answers with a partner.

Stereotypes about Scientists

All scientists use microscopes.

All scientists are men.

All scientists wear white coats.

Scientists don't play sports.

1. A stereotype is a _____ idea about a group of people that is not always true.
   a. bad
   b. common
   c. good

2. Can stereotypes hurt people? Can they help people?

3. Do you know any stereotypes?

MEET MIRNA VALERIO

A PREDICT What is a common stereotype about runners? Discuss with a partner.

B PHRASES TO KNOW Match the phrases from the video with the definitions.

1. _____ **lose weight**   a. to become thinner

2. _____ **be yourself**   b. to not act like someone else

C MAIN IDEAS Watch the video. Complete the sentence. ▶ 1.1

Mirna Valerio _____

a. looks like other runners.

b. runs far and fast.

c. shows that runners are all sizes.

D DETAILS Watch the video again. Check (✓) the things you hear about Mirna. ▶ 1.1

a. _____ She is a runner.

b. _____ Mirna is the stereotype of a runner.

c. _____ She does marathons.

d. _____ It is difficult for Mirna to run.

e. _____ Mirna runs to lose weight.

f. _____ She has a son.

g. _____ She runs for her health.

h. _____ Her goal is to be fast.

E What words do people sometimes connect to men and women? Discuss your answers in a small group.

Men _____sports_____

Women _____cook_____

F Look at the words you listed for your gender in activity E. Which are true for you? Which are not? Discuss in a small group.

Many people connect sports to men. This is true for me. I'm a man, and I like sports.

A stereotype is that women cook. That isn't true for me. I don't cook.

Say who you are and who you are not.

> You are going to reintroduce yourself (introduce yourself again) to the
> class. Use the ideas, vocabulary, and skills from the unit.

G MODEL Listen to a student introduce himself with three *I am* and two *I am not* sentences. Check the categories he talks about. 🎧 1.6

☐ age   ☐ country   ☐ not good at   ☐ free time   ☐ school

☐ gender   ☐ good at   ☐ personality   ☐ job   ☐ family

PRONUNCIATION   Consonants and voicing 🎧 1.7

Vowels (*a, e, i, o, u, y*) and consonants (***b, c, d, f, g, h, j, k, l, m, n, p, q, r, s, t, v, w, x, z***) make words.

Some consonants are voiced, or our throat vibrates when we say them (/d/, /v/). Others are voiceless. Our throat doesn't vibrate when we say them (/t/, /f/).

The following pairs of consonants are formed in the mouth the same way, but the voicing is different. Listen and repeat.

Voiced	Voiceless
/v/ ha**ve**	/f/ hal**f**
/g/ **g**oat	/k/ **c**oat
/b/ **b**at	/p/ **p**at
/z/ bu**zz**	/s/ bu**s**
/d/ sa**d**	/t/ sa**t**
/dʒ/ **J**ane	/tʃ/ **ch**ain

H PRONUNCIATION Listen and choose the words you hear. 🎧 1.8

1. pear / bear
2. leaf / leave
3. Sue / zoo
4. back / bag
5. to / do

6. come / gum
7. bat / bad
8. sip / zip
9. fan / van
10. cap / cab

I PRONUNCIATION Read the pairs. Then, with a partner, take turns saying one of the two words. Point to the word you hear.

1. pill   bill
2. ice   eyes
3. cold   gold
4. ant   and

5. choke   joke
6. safe   save
7. sip   zip
8. badge   batch

GRAMMAR Adjectives

Adjectives describe people, places, and things. They can come after the verb *be*. They can also come before nouns. Adjectives are never plural.

*Nadia **is tall**.*

*My sister **is quiet**.*

***Tall people** are common in my family.*

***Quiet people** are not all shy.*

J GRAMMAR Read the conversation. Underline all the adjectives. Check your answers with a partner.

A: Tell me about your brother and sister.

B: My brother is messy. His bedroom isn't clean. He's also noisy. He plays loud music all the time. But he is a fun brother. We play games together. He tells funny jokes.

A: What about your sister?

B: She's quiet. She's in her bedroom a lot. She's smart and is a good student. Math is easy for her, but it's difficult for me. She's kind and helps me with my homework.

K GRAMMAR Think of three adjectives to describe a classmate. Write them down. Then tell the class. Ask your classmates to guess who you're talking about.

This person is tall. She has black hair. She is funny. Who is she?

L PLAN Choose five categories. Write an *I am* statement for three categories. Write an *I am not* statement for two categories.

Age	
Country	
Free time	
Good at	
Personality	
Not good at	
Family	
Job	
School	

SPEAKING SKILL   Speak with confidence

When you speak, it's important to speak confidently.

To speak with confidence:

▸ Practice what you plan to say.
▸ Speak loudly and clearly.
▸ Look at the audience.

M PRACTICE Use your answers in activity L to prepare your introduction. Practice introducing yourself to a partner. Practice speaking confidently.

N UNIT TASK Reintroduce yourself to the class. Say who you are and who you are not.

REFLECT

A Check (✓) the Reflect activities you can do and the academic skills you can use.

☐ introduce yourself

☐ find things in common

☐ discuss stereotypes

☐ say who you are and who you are not

☐ predict

☐ speak with confidence

☐ simple present of *be*

☐ adjectives

☐ personalize

B Check (✓) the vocabulary words from the unit that you know. Circle words you still need to practice. Add any other words that you learned.

NOUN	VERB	ADJECTIVE	ADVERB & OTHER
free time	agree	fast	far
goal ᴬᵂ	be called	friendly	
idea	be interested in	hard	
job ᴬᵂ	believe	last	
size	matter	thin	
way	meet	wrong	
	smile		

C Reflect on the ideas in the unit as you answer these questions.

1. When do you need to make a good first impression?

_____

_____

2. What ideas and skills can you use from the unit?

_____

_____

WHAT IS HOME ?

SKILLS

LISTENING
Listen for main ideas

SPEAKING
Introduce a topic

GRAMMAR
Simple present

Simple present negative

CRITICAL THINKING
Categorize information

CONNECT TO THE TOPIC

1. What do you see in this home?
2. What do you have in your home?

A couple spends time at home in Bologna, Italy.

PREPARE TO LISTEN

A VOCABULARY Listen. Then choose a word to complete the sentences. 🎧 2.1

alone (adj)	during (prep)	move (v)	share (v)	sunny (adj)
comfortable (adj)	home (n)	(one's) own (adj)	space (n)	there (adv)

1. Our _____ isn't big, but I like it because I live _____ with my family.

2. My kitchen has a lot of windows. When it's a nice day, the room is very _____.

3. No one is at my house _____ the day. We are all at work or school.

4. I live _____ in my apartment. No other people live with me.

5. My house is small. There is not a lot of _____.

6. I _____ into my new house today. I am happy to be in a new house!

7. I study in my living room. I sit in a big chair. It is very _____. It feels good to sit in it.

8. My sister and I _____ a bathroom. It is hard. She is in the bathroom a lot!

9. I live with my brother in an apartment. We have our _____ bathrooms. It is very nice.

B Listen to someone talk about her new home. Complete the sentences with words from activity A. 🎧 2.2

I ¹_____ into a new apartment today. I live ²_____. My new ³_____ is small, but it is very ⁴_____. There are four rooms. There is a bedroom, a living room, a kitchen, and a bathroom. The living room is big and ⁵_____. I do many things in the living room ⁶_____ the day. I study in the living room. I eat in the living room. I watch TV in the living room. I live ⁷_____! I like having my ⁸_____ apartment. I don't ⁹_____ with anyone. I am happy in my new home!

C PERSONALIZE Choose the answers that are true for you. Then share your answers with a partner.

1. I live in **an apartment / a house / other**.

2. I live **alone / with my parents / with a partner (husband/wife) / with my sibling(s) (brother/sister) / with a roommate / other**.

3. There is **a lot / not a lot** of space.

4. There are **2 / 3 / 4 / 5 / 6 / other** rooms.

5. This is my **first / second / third / other** home.

REFLECT Explore reasons people move.

You are going to hear people talk about moving. Work with a small group. Complete the chart with the words. Do you know anyone in any of these situations?

alone	close	comfortable	move	own	space

Why People Move	
Family	▶ get married ▶ ¹_____ closer to parents
Change	▶ want to live ²_____ ▶ want to buy your ³_____ home ▶ want a home with more ⁴_____
Work	▶ get a new job ▶ be ⁵_____ to work
Other	▶ go to university ▶ for more ⁶_____ weather

MOVING IN AND MOVING OUT

Moving day at Harvard University, Cambridge, Massachusetts, USA

A PREDICT You will hear three conversations about people moving. Choose what you think the people will talk about. Then listen and check your answer. 🔊 2.3

a. Why they are moving

b. Where they are moving

c. Both a. and b.

LISTENING SKILL   Listen for main ideas

When you listen for the main ideas, you listen to understand the important information about the topic. Don't worry about understanding all the words. Listen for key words or important words. Listen for words that:

▶ the speaker says more than once.

▶ the speaker says more loudly and clearly.

▶ the speaker pauses on or says more slowly.

B APPLY Listen to the conversations again. Write the number of the conversation next to the home the people talk about. 🔊2.3

apartment _____   dorm room _____   house _____

C MAIN IDEAS Listen again. Match the people to the reasons they move. 🔊2.3

1. _____ Mariella   a. school

2. _____ Marcus   b. more space

3. _____ Zhanetta   c. new job

D DETAILS Listen again. Write T for *True* or F for *False*. 🔊2.3

Conversation 1

1. _____ Mariella moves on Sunday.

2. _____ She loves her new home.

3. _____ Her new home has a lot of space.

Conversation 2

1. _____ Marcus meets someone.

2. _____ This is Marcus's first time to live alone.

3. _____ Marcus doesn't want to live alone.

Conversation 3

1. _____ Zhanetta is a student.

2. _____ Students have their own bathrooms.

3. _____ There is a big space for students to sit and watch TV.

GRAMMAR   Simple present

We use the simple present to talk about routine activities and things that are true.

*I **love** my house. I **read** in the living room. My family **eats** dinner in the kitchen.*

Subject	Verb
I/You/We/They	love/read/eat
He/She/It	loves/reads/eats

For verbs that end in:

▸ voiceless sounds, say /s/—works, cooks, sleeps.
▸ voiced sounds, say /z/—listens, studies, plays.
▸ /s/, /ch/, /sh/, add *-es* and say /iz/—teaches, watches, washes.

E GRAMMAR Complete the sentences with the simple present of the verbs.

Carmen: I ¹_____ (study) in my bedroom. It's quiet there. My roommate is Mary. She
²_____ (talk) on the phone in the living room.

Joao: I have three roommates. We ³_____ (do) some things together and some
things alone. Omar ⁴_____ (read) in his bedroom. Andres ⁵_____
(listen) to music in his bedroom. Daniel ⁶_____ (play) video games in the living
room. We all ⁷_____ (eat) in the kitchen.

Hana: I ⁸_____ (live) alone. During the summer, I ⁹_____ (sit) in my yard.
The birds ¹⁰_____ (sing), and the sun ¹¹_____ (feel) warm on my
face. It's very comfortable.

Birds in a garden
in the UK

F Listen and check (✓) the sound you hear. Then practice saying each word. 🎧 2.4

	/s/	/z/	/iz/
1. moves			
2. makes			
3. watches			
4. drinks			
5. shares			
6. uses			
7. loves			
8. eats			

G Work with a partner. Ask your partner questions to complete your chart. Student A uses the chart below. Student B uses the chart on page 32.

A: What does Maddalena do in the bedroom?

B: She watches TV.

STUDENT A

	Bedroom	Living room	Kitchen
Robert	reads		
Maddalena	watches TV	eats	
Grace	studies		cooks

REFLECT	Ask about activities people do at home.

What do you do in your home? Where do you do the activities?

I _____ sing _____ in the _____ bathroom _____.

I _____ in the _____.

I _____ in the _____.

I _____ in the _____.

Talk to three classmates. Complete the chart with one activity and place for each classmate. Share the results with the class.

Name	Activity and place

PREPARE TO WATCH

Children play chess in Abu Dhabi, United Arab Emirates.

A VOCABULARY Listen to the words. Match the words with the definitions. 🎧 2.5

1. _____ chat (n)   a. a building, town, city, etc.

2. _____ cozy (adj)   b. a friendly talk

3. _____ holiday (n)   c. an important day (e.g., Independence Day)

4. _____ memory (n)   d. comfortable and warm

5. _____ place (n)   e. something you remember from the past

6. _____ present (adj)   f. to become happy and comfortable

7. _____ really (adv)   g. to believe someone or something

8. _____ relax (v)   h. very or very much

9. _____ smell (n)   i. what you notice with your nose

10. _____ trust (v)   j. in a particular place

B What word matches each description of home? Choose the best word.

| activity | food | pet |
| feeling | holiday | place |

1. _____ Home is playing games in the living room with my family.

2. _____ My house on Elm Street is my home.

3. _____ My grandmother's chicken and rice is home.

4. _____ New Year's with my family is home.

5. _____ Home is where there is a lot of love.

6. _____ Home is where my cat is.

C PERSONALIZE Work with a partner. Take turns asking and answering the questions.

1. What are important **holidays** for you? What do you do? What food do you eat?

2. What **memories** do you have of your childhood home?

3. How do you **relax** at home?

REFLECT Think about what makes a house a home.

You are going to watch a video about homes. Look at the graph. Which of these ideas are the same for you? Share with a partner.

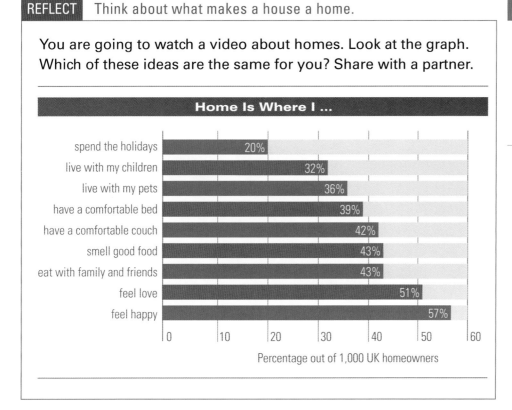

Home Is Where I ...

spend the holidays	20%
live with my children	32%
live with my pets	36%
have a comfortable bed	39%
have a comfortable couch	42%
smell good food	43%
eat with family and friends	43%
feel love	51%
feel happy	57%

0   10   20   30   40   50   60

Percentage out of 1,000 UK homeowners

We can use these questions to ask other people for their ideas.

What do you think?

What ideas do you have?

I think . . . What about you?

WATCH & SPEAK

WHAT IS
HOME TO YOU?

A father with his
children in Leli,
Georgia

A PREDICT Look at the title of the video and predict what it is about. Then watch the video and check your answer. ▶ 2.1

    a. Different ideas about homes

    b. Things in different homes

    c. Things people want in their homes

B PHRASES TO KNOW Choose the word or sentence that is most closely related to the phrase in **bold**.

    1. My best friend and I are not **blood-related**, but we feel like sisters.

       a. family   b. friend

    2. When I hear a good song, it **sticks with me**.

       a. I remember it.   b. I forget it.

C MAIN IDEAS Watch the video again and choose the main idea. ▶ 2.1

    a. Home is a place.

    b. Home is food and family.

    c. Home is many things.

D DETAILS Watch the video again. Check (✓) what people say home is. ▶ 2.1

a. _____ good friends	e. _____ my bed	i. _____ my living room
b. _____ food	f. _____ my dogs	j. _____ playing basketball
c. _____ holidays	g. _____ my dad	k. _____ watching movies
d. _____ memories	h. _____ my mom	l. _____ where I'm alone

CRITICAL THINKING Categorize information

Putting things in groups, or categories, helps us understand and remember information.

E APPLY What is an example of each category from the video?

    1. activity: _____   5. pet: _____

    2. food: _____   6. place: _____

    3. feeling: _____   7. thing: _____

    4. people: _____

Describe what home means to you.

You're going to describe what home means to you. Use the ideas, vocabulary, and skills from the unit.

F MODEL Listen to a student describe what her home means to her. Write a category from the box next to each sentence. Then answer the question. 🎧 2.6

activity	holiday	place
feeling	people	smell
food	pet	thing

1. _____ Home is my mother, father, and brother.

2. _____ It is my house in Toronto, Canada.

3. _____ It is my couch.

4. _____ I watch TV and read on my couch.

5. _____ Home is the smell of grass.

6. _____ Home is my mother's cookies.

7. _____ Home is my dog.

8. _____ I feel comfortable at home.

Which category does the student *not* talk about? _____

PRONUNCIATION Vowels 🎧 2.7

There are six vowels in English writing (*a, e, i, o, u,* and sometimes *y*), but there are 15 vowel sounds.

Each vowel can have more than one sound.

h**a**s /hæz/   sp**a**ce /speɪs/

Different vowels can also make the same vowel sounds.

m**ea**l /miʸl/   f**ee**l /fiʸl/   happ**y** /hæpiʸ/

---

30 UNIT 2

G PRONUNCIATION Listen to each set of words. Check (✓) if the vowel sound in **bold** is the same or different. 🎧 2.8

			Same	**Different**
1.	k**i**tchen	l**i**ving room	☐	☐
2.	r**oo**m	m**o**ve	☐	☐
3.	sp**a**ce	rel**a**x	☐	☐
4.	tog**e**ther	m**e**mories	☐	☐
5.	s**u**n	st**u**dent	☐	☐

H PRONUNCIATION Listen to each set of words. Choose the two words with the same vowel sound in **bold**. 🎧 2.9

1.	appl**y**	ch**i**ldhood	s**i**t
2.	h**o**me	r**o**ad	s**o**ck
3.	m**ai**l	m**ea**l	sl**ee**p
4.	gr**ea**t	pl**a**ce	h**a**t
5.	s**u**nlight	**u**niform	c**o**mfortable

GRAMMAR   Simple present negative

We use *do not* and *does not* before a verb to form the negative simple present. The contractions are *don't* and *doesn't*.

   I **don't study** in the living room. He **doesn't sleep** on the couch.

Subject	**Verb**
I/You/We/They	do not (don't) study/sleep/eat
He/She/It	does not (doesn't) study/sleep/eat

I GRAMMAR Complete the sentences with the simple present negative of the verbs.

1. My friends and I _____ (eat) in the dining room.

2. His roommate _____ (study) at home.

3. Maria and Lucia _____ (watch) TV in the bedroom.

4. My grandmother _____ (cook) in the kitchen.

5. My friends _____ (play) video games in the living room.

6. My apartment _____ (have) a lot of space.

J PLAN Think about your home. Write ideas for five or six categories. Think about photos and things from home that you can show.

Activity	Food	Feeling	People	Place	Thing

SPEAKING SKILL   Introduce a topic

When you give a presentation, it's important to introduce the topic clearly. Here are some ways to do this.

▶ One-sentence summary: *Home is many things to me.*
▶ General statement: *Home means different things to different people.*
▶ Question: *What does home mean to me?*

K APPLY Choose a way to introduce the topic of your presentation, and write it below.

_____

_____

L PRACTICE Use your notes from activities J and K to prepare your presentation. Practice giving your talk to a partner.

M UNIT TASK Tell your class what home means to you. Use photos and things from home to help you.

STUDENT B (chart for activity G on page 25)

	Bedroom	Living room	Kitchen
Robert		exercises	makes dinner
Maddalena	watches TV		washes the dishes
Grace		plays video games	

REFLECT

A Check (✓) the Reflect activities you can do and the academic skills you can use.

☐ explore reasons people move
☐ ask about activities people do at home
☐ think about what makes a house a home
☐ describe what home means to you

☐ listen for main ideas
☐ introduce a topic
☐ simple present
☐ simple present negative
☐ categorize information

B Check (✓) the vocabulary words from the unit that you know. Circle words you still need to practice. Add any other words that you learned.

NOUN	VERB	ADJECTIVE	ADVERB & OTHER
chat	move	alone	during
holiday	relax ᴬᵂ	comfortable	really
home	share	cozy	there
memory	trust	(one's) own	
place		present	
smell		sunny	
space			

C Reflect on the ideas in the unit as you answer these questions.

1. Are your classmates' ideas about home very different?

_____

_____

2. What ideas and skills from the unit can you use in the future?

_____

_____

TRACKING LIFE

A man uses a virtual training app.

CONNECT TO THE TOPIC

1. What is the man doing?

2. How do you know when you get better at an activity?

PREPARE TO WATCH

A VOCABULARY Listen to the words. Complete the sentences with the correct form of the words. 🎧 3.1

check (v)	every (adj)	kind (n)	show (v)	visit (v)
daily (adj)	get (v)	part (n)	travel (v)	water (n)

1. I think I have a new message. Let me _____.

2. My pet is an important _____ of my life. I love my cat!

3. When my brother moves out next week, I _____ his bedroom.

4. I need a new computer. I don't know what _____ to buy.

5. Marta and I are good friends. We _____ each other a lot.

6. I like to _____ to different countries. It's fun to see new places.

7. I love books. I read _____ day.

8. I take a _____ bike ride. I go every morning.

9. It is important to drink a lot of _____. I drink eight glasses a day.

10. I go to my grandmother's house on Sundays. She _____ me old family photos.

B Complete the chart with your own ideas.

Things I do daily	Things I use daily	Places I go every day	Things I check every day
read	phone	work	email

An early morning bike
ride in Denia, Spain

C Complete the sentences with the correct form of the words from activity A.
Then listen and check your answers. 🎧 3.2

Chi: I use my phone ¹_____ day. I ²_____ my email and social
media. I take photos and videos with my phone. I don't leave home without it!

Rashid: My father ³_____ a lot for work. He is a pilot. He flies planes.
He ⁴_____ a lot of different places and ⁵_____ me photos
and videos he takes.

Paula: On Fridays, I ⁶_____ two hours for lunch. I like to take a walk
along the ⁷_____. It is the best ⁸_____ of my week.

REFLECT Compare daily activities.

You are going to watch a video about daily life along the Mekong River.
Answer the questions in the chart with your own information. Then ask two
classmates the questions. Complete the chart with their information. Share
things you have in common.

	You	Classmate #1	Classmate #2
What do you do every morning?			
What do you do during the day?			
What do you do on weekends?			
What is the best part of your day?			

WATCH & SPEAK

LIFE ALONG THE MEKONG RIVER

A PREDICT David Guttenfelder is a National Geographic photographer. Look at the photo and read the caption. Answer the questions. Then watch the video and check your answers. ▶ 3.1

1. Who does Guttenfelder take photos of?

   a. Famous people

   b. Everyday people

2. What kind of things do the people do?

   a. Daily things

   b. Unusual things

B PHRASES TO KNOW Work with a partner. Discuss the meaning of these phrases from the video. Then take turns answering the questions.

1. What do you **take photos** of?

2. What things do you buy when you **go shopping**?

C MAIN IDEAS Watch the video again. What is the video about? ▶ 3.1

   a. The daily activities of David Guttenfelder during a trip to the Mekong River

   b. The daily activities of the people along the Mekong River

   c. Both a and b.

LISTENING SKILL   Listen for details

Details are the specific information about a topic. Details include names of people, kinds of things, dates and times, numbers, places, reasons, and examples. Listen for details to help you understand the main ideas.

D APPLY Watch the video again. Choose the correct answers. ▶ 3.1

1. Why does Guttenfelder go to the Mekong River?   **for fun / for his job**

2. What does one second in the video show?   **one day / one hour**

3. How many countries is the Mekong River in?   **many / one**

4. When do people use the Mekong River?   **every day / when they travel**

5. Who gets water for their plants?   **businesses / farmers**

6. Where do people sell things?   **at home / from their boats**

E DETAILS Who does each activity? Watch the video again. Write G for *Guttenfelder,* PM for *people along the Mekong,* or B for *both.* ▶ 3.1

1. _____ check camera

2. _____ get water

3. _____ go shopping

4. _____ sell things

5. _____ take a boat

6. _____ take a plane

7. _____ take photos

8. _____ talk to people

Photo of Phong Dien
floating market in Vietnam
by David Guttenfelder

GRAMMAR   Adverbs of frequency

We use adverbs of frequency to say how often we do something. They can come before most verbs.

100% ▲	I **always** drink coffee in the morning.
90%	I **usually** study in the library.
50%	I **sometimes** play video games.
5%	I **rarely** eat at a restaurant.
0% ▼	I **never** watch TV.

We can also use *usually* and *sometimes* at the beginning of a sentence.

Usually, I study in the library. **Sometimes**, I study at home.

F GRAMMAR Listen to Gina and Marcus talk about their daily activities. Write *G* for Gina or *M* for Marcus for how often they do each activity. Then compare answers with a partner. 🔊 3.3

	Wake up early	Go to a café	Check phone	Relax	Cook
always					
usually					
sometimes					
rarely					
never					

CRITICAL THINKING   Make comparisons

When we compare things, we say how they are the same or different. This helps you understand a topic better. For example, if you compare your daily activities to a friend's, you learn more about your own life.

*Omar and Cesar are **the same**. They **both** wake up early.*
*Junko and Li are **different**. Junko always eats out, **but** Li rarely does.*

Friends at a café in Stockholm, Sweden

G GRAMMAR Ask three classmates how often they do the activities. Write their names. Then work with a partner and make comparisons.

How often do you . . . ?

	Always	Usually	Sometimes	Rarely	Never
wake up early					
use your phone in class					
see friends					
watch TV					
cook					
play sports					

REFLECT Analyze your free time.

Work with a small group. Look at the chart. What does the chart show? How does the way you use your free time compare with this chart?

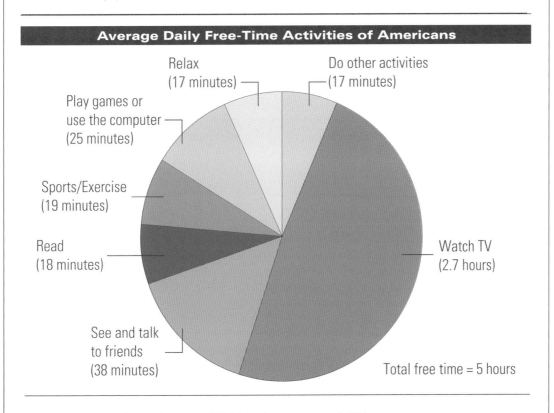

Average Daily Free-Time Activities of Americans

Relax (17 minutes)
Do other activities (17 minutes)
Play games or use the computer (25 minutes)
Sports/Exercise (19 minutes)
Read (18 minutes)
Watch TV (2.7 hours)
See and talk to friends (38 minutes)
Total free time = 5 hours

Americans watch 2.7 hours of TV, but I never watch TV.

PREPARE TO LISTEN

A VOCABULARY Listen to the words in **bold**. Match the words with their definitions. 🎧 3.4

1. _____ She writes in her **diary** every day.

2. _____ He always does his **exercises** in the evening. His legs are strong.

3. _____ I like mornings. I **feel** happy in the morning.

4. _____ She wakes up early every morning. It's a **habit**.

5. _____ I don't drink coffee. I drink tea **instead**.

6. _____ A baby's first word is an important **moment**.

7. _____ We go outside **more** in the summer.

8. _____ My roommate walks every morning. I walk **too**, sometimes.

9. _____ I **track** my sleep with an app. It shows me how many hours I sleep.

10. _____ Let's **try** a new restaurant today.

a. (adv) also

b. (n) an activity you always do

c. (v) to do something different or new

d. (n) a book where you write your thoughts

e. (v) to record an activity

f. (n) time

g. (adv) a greater amount

h. (n) an activity you do to be healthy and strong

i. (adv) in place of something

j. (v) to experience an emotion

B PERSONALIZE Discuss the questions in a small group.

1. Do you write in a **diary**?

2. Do you do any **exercise**?

3. When do you **feel** happy?

4. What is something you are doing **more** now?

5. What is something you want to **try**?

> ### COMMUNICATION TIP
>
> Use these phrases to show interest during a conversation.
>
> *Really?*
>
> *Why (not)?*
>
> *That's interesting.*
>
> *Tell me more about . . .*

On a walk in Auckland, New Zealand

C Look at the activities Mary tracks. Then answer the questions. Work with a small group.

1. What activities does Mary track?
2. Which activities does Mary track every day?
3. On what days does Mary track her sleep?
4. Does Mary get enough sleep?
5. Why does Mary track her steps?

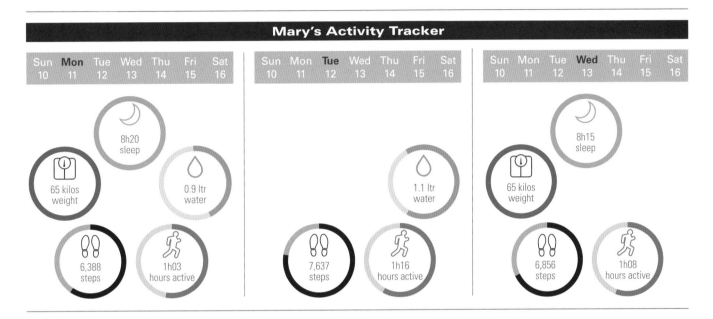

Mary's Activity Tracker

| Sun 10 | **Mon 11** | Tue 12 | Wed 13 | Thu 14 | Fri 15 | Sat 16 |

8h20 sleep
65 kilos weight
0.9 ltr water
6,388 steps
1h03 hours active

| Sun 10 | Mon 11 | **Tue 12** | Wed 13 | Thu 14 | Fri 15 | Sat 16 |

1.1 ltr water
7,637 steps
1h16 hours active

| Sun 10 | Mon 11 | Tue 12 | **Wed 13** | Thu 14 | Fri 15 | Sat 16 |

8h15 sleep
65 kilos weight
6,856 steps
1h08 hours active

REFLECT Evaluate your habits.

You will hear a conversation about apps that track daily activities. Think about some habits you have. Complete the chart. Then compare with a partner.

Good habits	Bad habits
I walk to work every day.	I don't drink water during the day.

LISTEN & SPEAK

HABITS AND APPS

A PREVIEW What tracking apps do you know? Brainstorm or look up some ideas for each category with a partner.

Food/drink apps	Exercise apps	Other

B MAIN IDEAS Listen to the conversation. What three apps do they talk about? Write them in the chart in activity A. 🎧 3.5

C DETAILS Listen again. Write T for *True* or F for *False*. 🎧 3.5

App 1

1. _____ The app tracks how much water she drinks.

2. _____ The app tells her to drink more water.

3. _____ She doesn't drink more water now.

App 2

4. _____ The app tracks how much time he walks.

5. _____ He usually takes 10,000 steps every day.

6. _____ He takes the elevator instead of the stairs now.

App 3

7. _____ The app tracks the food she eats.

8. _____ She adds photos to the app.

9. _____ She tries to use the app every day.

D Discuss the questions in a small group.

1. Do you want to try any of the apps from the conversation?
2. Which app from the conversation takes the most time to use? Which takes the least?
3. What is good about a tracking app? What is bad?

E Choose a habit you want to change. Answer the questions. Then track your habit starting today.

1. Right now I _____, but I want to _____.

2. How do you want to track your habit? Check one or more.
   ☐ an app   ☐ paper and pencil   ☐ photographs   ☐ video

Tourists check their phones
in London, England.

Give a talk about a habit you want to change.

You are going to give a presentation about tracking a habit. Use the ideas, vocabulary, and skills from the unit.

SPEAKING SKILL Give reasons

We give reasons to explain things. The word *because* often introduces a reason. The part of the sentence with *because* can come at the beginning or the end of a sentence.

> I wake up early every day **because** I go to work at 7 a.m.
> **Because** he has sleep problems, he uses a sleep app.

F MODEL Listen to someone talk about tracking her sleep. Then answer the questions. 🎧 3.6

1. Why does she want to change her sleep habit? _____

2. Why does she go to bed late? _____

G APPLY Match the reason to the activity.

1. _____ I walk every day   a. because it isn't quiet. Her family is loud!

2. _____ She doesn't study at home   b. because they like to be outside.

3. _____ He uses a water app   c. because I don't have time during the week.

4. _____ I visit my parents on the weekend   d. because I am tired.

5. _____ They eat lunch at the park   e. because he wants to drink more water.

6. _____ I never go places on the weekend   f. because I sit too much at work.

PRONUNCIATION Syllables 🎧 3.7

All words have one or more syllables. A syllable can be one vowel sound or one vowel sound plus one or more consonant sounds. You can use a dictionary to check how many syllables a word has.

1 syllable	2 syllables	3 syllables
cook	stu•dy	ex•er•cise
lunch	wa•ter	com•put•er
track	vis•it	un•der•stand

H PRONUNCIATION Write the words you hear. Then write the number of syllables in each word. Practice saying the words. 🎧 3.8

Word	# of syllables	Word	# of syllables	Word	# of syllables
1.		4.		7.	
2.		5.		8.	
3.		6.		9.	

I PRONUNCIATION Decide if the two words in each pair have the same number of syllables. Write S for *Same* or D for *Different*. Then listen and check your answers. 🎧 3.9

1. _____ friendly / holiday   3. _____ important / instead   5. _____ memory / activity

2. _____ feeling / hobby   4. _____ habit / change   6. _____ daily / diary

---

GRAMMAR   Prepositions of time

We use prepositions of time to say when we do something.

Use **at** for specific times.

> *Class starts **at** 9:00. **At** noon, I eat lunch.*

Use **on** for days and dates.

> *The farmer's market opens **on** Saturday. It closes **on** September 23.*

Use **in** for months, years, seasons, and times of day (except **noon** and **night**).

> *School starts **in** September. I graduate **in** the spring **in** 2025!*

J GRAMMAR Complete the sentences with a preposition of time.

1. I have geography class every Friday _____ 9:00 _____ the morning.

2. _____ the first Friday of every month, we begin a new unit.

3. I read more about the places we study _____ Saturdays and Sundays.

4. I think the best time to go to Vietnam is _____ the dry season.

5. The dry season starts _____ December and ends _____ April.

6. We usually go outside _____ noon and come back _____ 1:00 p.m.

K GRAMMAR Tell your partner what you do at these times.

1. 11:00 a.m. / weekdays   *I work at 11:00 a.m. on weekdays.*
2. Saturdays
3. Friday / evenings
4. Summer
5. January 1st

L PLAN Complete the outline with information about tracking your habit.

Today, I'm going to talk about tracking _____.

I always / usually / sometimes / rarely / never _____.

I want to change this habit because _____

_____.

I want to _____ instead.

I use _____ to track _____.

I notice I _____

_____.

M PRACTICE Use your outline from activity L to prepare your presentation. Practice giving your talk to a partner.

N UNIT TASK Give a presentation about tracking a habit. Use the chart to take notes about three classmates. Copy the chart in your notebook if you need more space. In small groups, discuss things people have in common.

Name	Habit	Reason	How to track

REFLECT

A Check (✓) the Reflect activities you can do and the academic skills you can use.

☐ compare daily activities

☐ analyze your free time

☐ evaluate your habits

☐ give a talk about a habit you want to change

☐ listen for details

☐ give reasons

☐ adverbs of frequency

☐ prepositions of time

☐ make comparisons

B Check (✓) the vocabulary words from the unit that you know. Circle words you still need to practice. Add any other words that you learned.

NOUN	VERB	ADJECTIVE	ADVERB & OTHER
diary AW	check	daily	instead
exercise	feel	every	more
habit	get		too
kind	show		
moment	track		
part	travel		
water	try		
	visit		

C Reflect on the ideas in the unit as you answer these questions.

1. Do you want to continue to track your habit? Explain.

_____

_____

2. What ideas will you use from the unit?

_____

_____

UNIT
4 | FOOD MATTERS

Palazzo del Freddo in Rome is one of the oldest ice-cream shops in Italy.

IN THIS UNIT

- ▶ Compare eating habits
- ▶ Explore how food connects you to others
- ▶ Define what a comfort food is
- ▶ Describe your comfort food

SKILLS

LISTENING
Listen for examples

SPEAKING
Use questions

GRAMMAR
Infinitives and gerunds

Sentences with *when*

CRITICAL THINKING
Make inferences

CONNECT TO THE TOPIC

1. What is the man holding?
2. Why is food important for us?

PREPARE TO LISTEN

A ACTIVATE List the food words you know for each category.

Fruit	Vegetable	Meat	Other

B VOCABULARY Listen to the words. Complete the conversations with the correct form of the words. Then read the conversations with a partner. 🔊4.1

bring (v)	delicious (adj)	hungry (adj)	recipe (n)	sick (adj)
connect (v)	dessert (n)	meal (n)	restaurant (n)	special (adj)

1. **A:** Do you eat breakfast with your family?

    B: No, the only _____ we eat together is dinner.

2. **A:** Do you do something _____ for your birthday?

    B: My mother always makes a cake, but she tries a new

    _____ every year. All her cakes are

    _____.

    A: Yum! I love cakes and other _____.

3. **A:** Food is important in my family. We like cooking together.

    B: That's a nice way to _____ with your family.

4. **A:** I'm usually very _____ in the morning.

    B: I am, too! I always eat a big breakfast.

5. **A:** I don't want to cook tonight. I'm tired.

    B: Let's go eat at a _____. There's a new sushi

    place. Do you want to go there?

6. **A:** I don't feel well today.

    B: Oh, I'm sorry you're _____. Do you want me to

    _____ you some soup?

C PERSONALIZE Discuss the questions in a group.

1. What do you like to eat at **restaurants**?
2. How often do you eat **dessert**?
3. What are some **special** foods in your country?
4. How many **meals** do you eat every day?

D Complete the chart. Then compare your answers in a group.

	When do you eat?	Where do you eat?	What do you eat?	Who do you eat with?
Breakfast				
Lunch				
Dinner				

REFLECT Compare eating habits.

You will hear a radio show about how food connects people. Read the infographic. Discuss the questions with a partner.

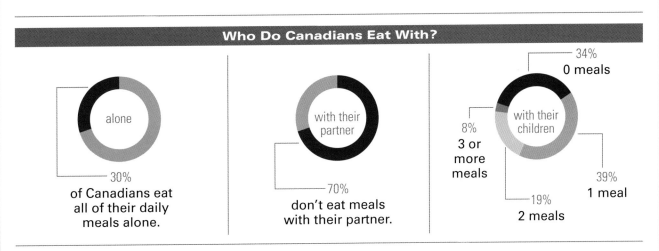

Who Do Canadians Eat With?

30% of Canadians eat all of their daily meals alone.

70% don't eat meals with their partner.

with their children: 34% 0 meals, 8% 3 or more meals, 19% 2 meals, 39% 1 meal

1. What percent of Canadians eat their daily meals alone?
2. What percent of Canadians don't eat meals with their partner?
3. Do more Canadians eat meals with their children or not?
4. How do your eating habits compare with these numbers?

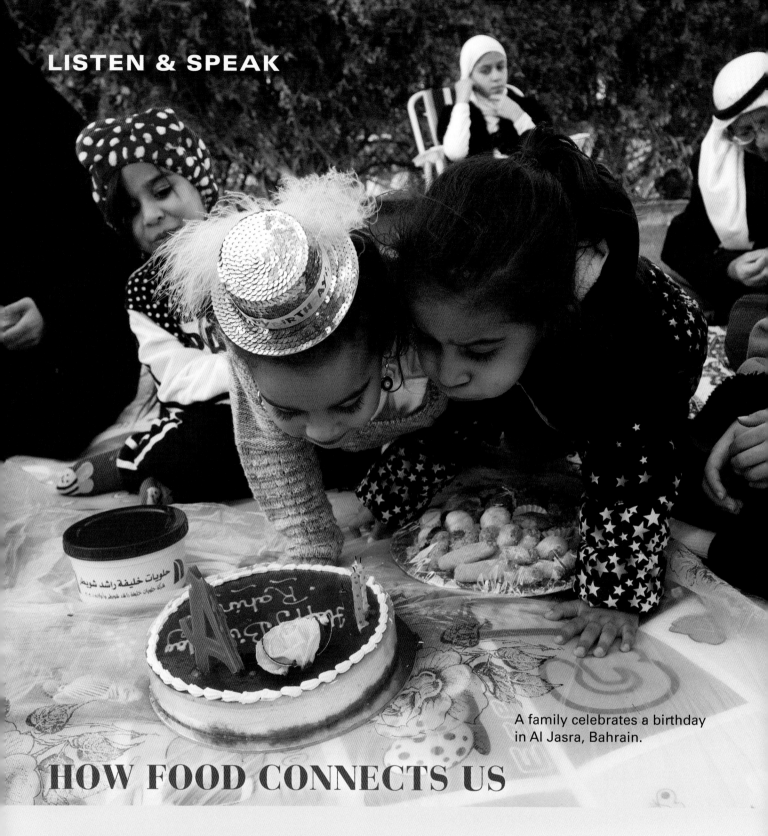

LISTEN & SPEAK

A family celebrates a birthday in Al Jasra, Bahrain.

HOW FOOD CONNECTS US

A PREDICT Match each group of people to one way you think food connects them. Then listen and check your answers. 🎧 4.2

1. _____ family   a.   at meals

2. _____ neighbors   b.   helping sick people

3. _____ new people   c.   restaurant groups

54 UNIT 4

B PHRASES TO KNOW Work with a partner. Discuss the meaning of these phrases from the radio show. Then take turns answering the questions.

1. What is your favorite **home-cooked meal**? Who makes it?
2. Uber **drops** people **off**. What does Uber Eats drop off?

C MAIN IDEAS What is the main idea of the radio show?

a. Food connects people with common interests.
b. Food connects people who live in the same place.
c. Food connects people in many ways.

D DETAILS Listen to the radio show again. Choose the correct answers. 🎧4.2

1. Ana Lucia's family likes to make a big meal every _____.

   a. Friday   b. Saturday   c. Sunday

2. Food connects Ana Lucia to her _____.

   a. family   b. school   c. work

3. Tony and his _____ make food for people who are sick.

   a. family   b. friends   c. neighbors

4. They buy food from the store or _____.

   a. cook something   b. bring them to a restaurant   c. give them a recipe

5. William joins a _____ group when he moves to a new city.

   a. cooking   b. neighbor   c. restaurant

6. The group chooses a different _____ every week.

   a. dessert   b. recipe   c. restaurant

LISTENING SKILL   Listen for examples

We use examples to make our ideas clear. Listen for these words and phrases that introduce examples.

*People are often busy with things **like** work and school.*

*Eating healthy food, **such as** fruits and vegetables, is important.*

*There are many kinds of restaurants. **For example**, there are Italian and Chinese ones.*

E APPLY Listen to an excerpt from the radio show. Who uses each word or phrase to introduce an example? Write A for *Ana Lucia* or T for *Tony*. 🎧4.3

1. _____ like

2. _____ for example

3. _____ such as

F APPLY Listen again. Choose the things each person gives examples of. 🎧4.3

Ana Lucia

a. desserts

b. recipes

c. restaurants

d. special days

Tony

a. bringing food to neighbors

b. special foods

c. where to buy food

GRAMMAR   Infinitives and gerunds

We use infinitives and gerunds to talk about activities.

Infinitive: *to* + verb	**Gerund: verb + *-ing***
I like **to eat** pizza.	We enjoy **meeting** new people.
He wants **to make** spaghetti.	She avoids **eating** junk food.

We use infinitives and gerunds with certain verbs.

Verbs + infinitive	**Verbs + gerund**	**Verbs + infinitive or gerund**	
learn	avoid	begin	love
need	dislike	hate	start
plan	enjoy	like	try
want			

G GRAMMAR Listen. Choose the infinitive or gerund you hear. 🎧4.4

1. to go / going

2. to eat / eating

3. to bake / baking

4. to join / joining

5. to buy / buying

6. to make / making

7. to cook / cooking

8. to take / taking

9. to have / having

10. to join / joining

H GRAMMAR Complete the conversation with an infinitive or a gerund. Sometimes both are correct. Then practice the conversation with a partner.

Farah: Next weekend is Sam's birthday. I need ¹_____ (plan) a party.

Li: I want ²_____ (help).

Farah: Thanks! Let's think about food. Sam enjoys ³_____ (cook).

Li: Oh, that's right. He takes a pizza-making class on Monday nights. He learns ⁴_____ (make) a different kind of pizza every week.

Farah: So, let's have a pizza party. We can all try ⁵_____ (make) our own pizzas.

Li: Fun! Games are fun, too. Do you want ⁶_____ (play) any games?

Farah: Sure, Sam likes ⁷_____ (play) games.

Li: Great. I have some games I can bring.

I GRAMMAR Write sentences about yourself. Use an infinitive or gerund. Then share your answers with a partner.

I enjoy _eating outside_____.

I like _____.

I want _____.

I need _____.

REFLECT   Explore how food connects you to others.

What events bring people and food together? Look at the examples in the chart and add your ideas. Then share your ideas with a small group.

Event	Who	Special food
birthday party	friends and family	birthday cake

A birthday party brings friends and family together. People like to eat cake at a birthday party.

PREPARE TO WATCH

A ACTIVATE Listen to the words. Put a check (✓) next to the ones you know. 🎧 4.5

healthy (adj)	normal (adj)	salty (adj)	spicy (adj)	sweet (adj)
maybe (adv)	sad (adj)	snack (n)	stressed (adj)	tired (adj)

B VOCABULARY Match the parts of the conversations.

1. _____ I'm hungry.
2. _____ I have a big test tomorrow.
3. _____ I eat a lot of fruits and vegetables.
4. _____ Our cooking class is over.
5. _____ Do you like these chips?
6. _____ What do you usually eat in the morning?
7. _____ Do you like cookies and cake?
8. _____ Is there any kind of food you don't like?
9. _____ Do you want to watch a movie with me?
10. _____ No one is in the restaurant.

a. Those are **healthy** things to eat.
b. No, they're too **salty**. I need some water now.
c. A **normal** breakfast for me is coffee and toast.
d. **Maybe** it's not open now.
e. Are you ready, or are you **stressed**?
f. I don't like **spicy** food. It hurts my mouth.
g. I'm **sad**. Let's take another one.
h. No, I'm **tired**. I need to go to bed.
i. Yes! I love **sweet** things.
j. Dinner is soon, so have a **snack** now.

C PERSONALIZE Answer the questions with a partner.

1. What are examples of **sweet**, **salty**, and **spicy** foods?
2. What is a **healthy snack**?
3. What is a **normal** breakfast for you?

D Complete the sentences with the words you hear. 🎧 4.6

There is a relationship between food and feelings. Some eating habits, like not

eating breakfast, can make us feel ¹_____. And some feelings can

make us want to eat food that isn't ²_____. For example, when

we feel ³_____ or ⁴_____, we want to eat something

⁵_____ or ⁶_____ to make us feel better.

CRITICAL THINKING Make inferences

When we use information to guess something, we infer. For example, imagine you are at a restaurant with a friend. As he eats, his face is red and he drinks a lot of water. You infer his food is spicy.

E APPLY Work with a partner. What can you infer about each situation?

1. Tanya always eats chocolate when she's stressed. You know she has a test today. You see her with chocolate.
2. Sandra never eats dessert, chips, or fried food. She always eats vegetables and fruit.
3. Maxim eats at a restaurant every night. He never cooks.
4. Henri rarely eats soup. He eats soup when he is sick. You see him with soup today.

REFLECT   Define what a comfort food is.

You will watch a podcast about *comfort food*. Read the definition of *comfort*. Then discuss with a partner what you think a comfort food is. Give examples.

comfort (n) something that makes you feel good

A plate of poutine, a Canadian dish

COMFORT FOODS

Firefighters in
Colorado, USA, take
a break to eat pizza.

A PREDICT What kind of foods are comfort foods? Choose the words that you think describe comfort foods. Then watch the podcast and check your answers. ▶4.1

1. They are **healthy / unhealthy** foods.

2. They are **normal / special** foods.

B PHRASES TO KNOW Discuss the meaning of the phrases from the video with a partner. Then answer the questions.

1. Sam goes to a coffee shop **for a little while** every day. He only stays for 15 minutes. What is something you do **for a little while** every day?

2. Abdul is very hungry. He wants to eat **right now**. What do you want to do **right now**?

C MAIN IDEAS Watch the video again. Choose the two main ideas. ▶4.1

a. _____ We feel good before we eat comfort foods.

b. _____ We feel good after we eat comfort foods.

c. _____ Usually, people from the same country have different comfort foods.

d. _____ Usually, people from the same country have the same comfort foods.

D DETAILS Watch an excerpt from the video. Match the comfort foods to the countries. ▶4.2

1. _____ poutine   a. Canada

2. _____ tortilla española   b. Egypt

3. _____ oden   c. Greece

4. _____ shakshouka   d. Italy

5. _____ baklava   e. Japan

6. _____ tiramisù   f. Spain

7. _____ apple pie   g. the United States

E What sweet, spicy, salty, or healthy foods do you like? Do you make them or buy them? Share your answers with a partner.

Describe your comfort food.

You are going to talk about your comfort food and who it connects you to. Use the ideas, vocabulary, and skills from the unit.

F MODEL Listen to a student describe his comfort food. Complete each part of the outline with no more than two words. 🎧 4.7

Comfort food: _____

Kind of food: _____

Eats it when he feels: _____

Eats it with: _____

Connects him to his: _____

SPEAKING SKILL Use questions

You can use questions to connect with the people you talk to. Here are two types of questions from the radio show and the video.

Questions other people answer:

Andy: How does food connect you to other people?
Ana Lucia: My family enjoys cooking together.

Questions the speaker answers:

Comfort food. What is it? To feel comfort means to feel good. So comfort food is food that makes us feel good.

G APPLY Listen again. Are these questions other people answer or questions the speaker answers? Write O for *Other* or S for *Speaker*. 🎧 4.7

1. _____ What is my comfort food?

2. _____ Who wants to eat ice cream with me after class?

PRONUNCIATION   Word stress 🔊 4.8

Many words have more than one syllable. We usually stress one of the
syllables more clearly. This means we say it a little longer, clearer, and louder
than the other syllables.

heal•thy   co•**nnect**   **re**•ci•pe   to•**ge**•ther

H   PRONUNCIATION Listen to the words. Underline the syllable that is
stressed. 🔊 4.9

1. spe•cial   3. sal•ty   5. heal•thy   7. ex•am•ple

2. de•li•cious   4. home•sick   6. spi•cy   8. hun•gry

I   PRONUNCIATION Write the number of syllables in each word. Then
write which syllable is stressed.

Word	Number of syllables	Syllable we stress
1. comfort	2	1
2. dessert		
3. exercise		
4. excited		
5. feeling		
6. holiday		
7. important		
8. restaurant		
9. tired		
10. normal		

GRAMMAR Sentences with *when*

We use *when* to talk about specific times and situations.

> **When I am sick**, I eat chicken soup. I feel better **when I eat this**.

A sentence with *when* has two parts. Each part has a subject and a verb. The part of the sentence with *when* can come at the beginning of the sentence or the end, but it cannot be a sentence by itself.

>   S V   S V
> **When I am tired**, I drink coffee.

>   S V   S V
> I drink coffee **when I am tired**.

J GRAMMAR Complete the first two sentences. Then write three more sentences with *when* about you or someone you know. Use the words and phrases below. Share your answers with a partner.

alone	happy	sick
listen to music	talk with friends	watch TV

1. When I am stressed, _____.

2. When I'm tired, _____.

3. _____

4. _____

5. _____

K PLAN Complete the outline with information about your comfort food.

Comfort food: _____

Kind of food: _____

I eat it when I feel: _____

I eat it with: _____

It connects me to my: _____

L PRACTICE Use your outline from activity K to prepare your presentation. Practice giving your talk to a partner.

M UNIT TASK Describe your comfort food in a small group. Bring the food or a photo of the food to share. Decide which comfort food sounds the best.

REFLECT

A Check (✓) the Reflect activities you can do and the academic skills you can use.

☐ compare eating habits

☐ explore how food connects you to others

☐ define what a comfort food is

☐ describe your comfort food

☐ listen for examples

☐ use questions

☐ infinitives and gerunds

☐ sentences with *when*

☐ make inferences

B Check (✓) the vocabulary words from the unit that you know. Circle words you still need to practice. Add any other words you learned.

NOUN	VERB	ADJECTIVE	ADVERB & OTHER
dessert	bring	delicious	maybe
meal	connect	healthy	
recipe ᴬᵂ		hungry	
restaurant		normal ᴬᵂ	
snack		sad	
		salty	
		sick	
		special	
		spicy	
		stressed ᴬᵂ	
		sweet	
		tired	

C Reflect on the ideas in the unit as you answer these questions.

1. How can you connect with the people around you through food?

_____

_____

2. What ideas or skills in this unit can you use in the future?

_____

_____

5 | MORE THAN A GAME

The Tour of Oman

IN THIS UNIT

▸ Categorize sports

▸ Explore opinions about sports

▸ Discuss uncommon sports

▸ Debate if an activity is a sport or not

SKILLS

LISTENING
Listen for opinions

SPEAKING
Use listing words and phrases

GRAMMAR
Gerunds

Conjunctions *and* and *but*

CRITICAL THINKING
Brainstorm

CONNECT TO THE TOPIC

1. What is the Tour of Oman?

2. What sports are common in your country?

PREPARE TO LISTEN

A VOCABULARY Listen to the words. Complete the conversations with the correct form of the words. Then practice the conversations with a partner. 🎧 5.1

against (prep)	player (n)	ride (v)	skill (n)	whole (adj)
physical (adj)	practice (v)	rule (n)	team (n)	win (v)

1. **A:** Do you have a good basketball _____?

   B: No. We have a lot of new _____. We need to learn how to play together.

2. **A:** Do you want to play chess with me?

   B: Are you sure you want to play _____ me? I'm really good at chess.

3. **A:** Do you like to watch basketball?

   B: Not really. There are so many _____. I don't know them all.

4. **A:** Do you like to play American football?

   B: It is fun to watch. But I don't want to play it. It's a very _____ game. You use your _____ body.

5. **A:** When is your volleyball game?

   B: It's tomorrow. I hope we _____!

6. **A:** You are really good at soccer.

   B: Thank you. I _____ two hours every day.

7. **A:** Golf is a fun sport.

   B: I agree. My _____ are not great, but I like to play.

8. **A:** Do you always _____ your bike to work?

   B: Yes, it gives me some exercise before and after work.

B PERSONALIZE Discuss the questions in a small group.

1. Why is it important to follow the **rules** in sports?
2. What do you do that is **physical**? What do you do that is not very **physical**?
3. What **skills** are important in soccer?

A sports field at the Colégio Santo Agostinho Nova Lima in Belo Horizonte, Brazil

C   Match the quotes about sports with their meanings. Then discuss the quotes with a partner. Do you agree or disagree?

1. _____ "It's not the team with the best players that wins. It's the players with the best team that wins."

2. _____ "Practice makes perfect."

3. _____ "Winning isn't everything. But wanting to win is."

a.   Players on a team need to work together to win.

b.   It's OK to not win as long as you try hard.

c.   You need to do something again and again to get better at it.

CRITICAL THINKING   Brainstorm

When you brainstorm, you think of as many ideas as possible. No ideas are bad. You write all ideas down and decide which ones to use later. Brainstorming helps you think of things in different ways and be creative.

REFLECT   Categorize sports.

You are going to hear a class discussion about sports. Look at the chart. Brainstorm more categories of sports. Then think of sports and put them in the categories.

Sports with teams	Sports with one player		
soccer	tennis		

LISTEN & SPEAK
WHAT IS A SPORT?

A PREVIEW Look at the photo and read the caption. Answer the questions.

1. What are the men doing?
2. What do you know about this sport?
3. Do players do this in other sports?

B MAIN IDEAS Listen to the class discussion. Check (✓) the three main ideas. 🎧 5.2

a. _____ A sport is a game with rules and physical exercise.

b. _____ Playing sports is healthy.

c. _____ Some people disagree about which activities are sports.

d. _____ Soccer, basketball, and baseball are common sports.

e. _____ There are different kinds of sports.

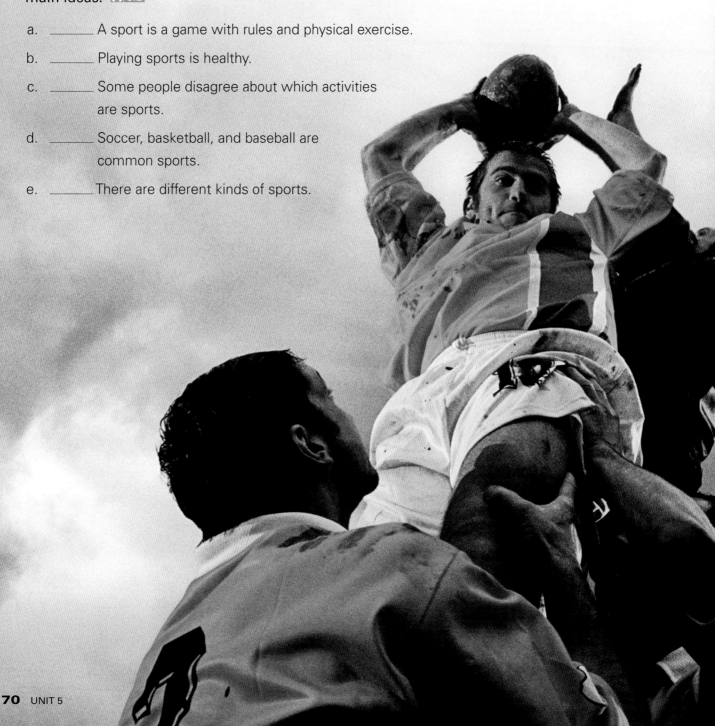

C PHRASES TO KNOW Complete the conversation with phrases from the class discussion.

each other	hold on	how about ...?

A: Do you want to play tennis now? We need one more player.

B: Sure! But I'm not very good.

A: That's OK. We aren't good, either. But we help [1]_____.

B: OK, [2]_____. I need to get my shoes.

A: [3]_____ your tennis racket? You need that, too.

D DETAILS Listen to an excerpt from the class discussion. Check (✓) all the examples you hear. 🎧 5.3

- ☐ baseball
- ☐ basketball
- ☐ chess
- ☐ e-gaming
- ☐ golf
- ☐ hockey
- ☐ horse racing
- ☐ karate
- ☐ martial arts
- ☐ running
- ☐ skiing
- ☐ soccer
- ☐ swimming
- ☐ tennis
- ☐ track
- ☐ volleyball

Young men playing rugby

An opinion is something a person thinks or believes. It's important to listen for opinions. Listen for phrases like these. Note that you can drop *that*, especially in speaking.

> **I think (that)** golf is fun to play. **I don't think** it's fun to watch.
> **I believe (that)** everyone should play a sport. **I feel** exercise is important.
> **In my opinion,** yoga is not a sport.

Other words can also show a person's opinion. Listen for verbs such as *enjoy*, *hate*, *like*, and *love*. Listen for adjectives such as *bad*, *beautiful*, *boring*, *good*, *fun*, and *ugly*.

> I **love** golf. It's **fun** to play.

E APPLY Listen to another excerpt from the class discussion. Put the phrases and words in the order you hear them (1–4). 🎧5.4

_____ But, in my opinion . . .   _____ . . . fun

_____ I think . . .   _____ I disagree.

GRAMMAR Gerunds

A gerund is the *-ing* form of a verb. It acts like a noun. Like other nouns, gerunds can be the subject or object in a sentence.

Gerund as a subject	Gerund as an object
Exercising is fun.	I love **exercising**.
Car racing is boring.	I don't like **car racing**.
Winning feels good.	I enjoy **winning** volleyball games.

F GRAMMAR Complete each sentence with a gerund. Then write S if the gerund is the *subject* of the sentence or O if it is the *object*.

1. In my opinion, _____ (win) is not important.   _____

2. _____ (know) the rules is an important part of a sport.   _____

3. _____ (meet) new people is a great part of sports.   _____

4. Roberto likes _____ (practice) every day.   _____

5. _____ (spend) time together as a team is important.   _____

6. Yuko hates _____ (play) soccer when it's hot.   _____

7. I always enjoy _____ (learn) new games.   _____

G GRAMMAR Listen to three people. Complete the sentences with the gerunds you hear. 5.5

Katrina: ¹_____ is my sport! ²_____ to the swim meets is a lot of fun. But ³_____ is not fun. I don't like ⁴_____ in the water for three hours every day.

Abbas: ⁵_____ hockey is my favorite thing to do. I like ⁶_____ my favorite players. They are very fast on the ice. My friends and I enjoy ⁷_____ at a restaurant and watching games together.

An: I love ⁸_____ time with my family. ⁹_____ games together is my favorite activity. Sometimes I win and sometimes I lose. I like ¹⁰_____ more!

REFLECT Explore opinions about sports.

Look at the chart. Discuss the questions with a partner.

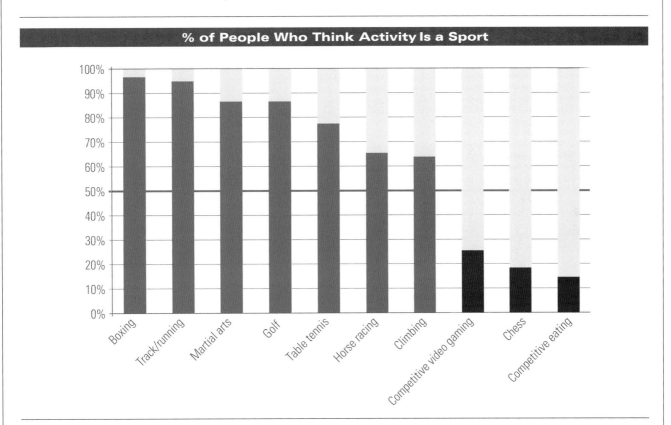

% of People Who Think Activity Is a Sport

1. What does the chart show?
2. How many activities are in the chart?
3. Which activities do most people think are sports?
4. Which activities do most people think are not sports?
5. Which activities do you think are sports? Which are not? Explain.

PREPARE TO WATCH

A VOCABULARY Listen to the words. Match each word with a definition. Use a dictionary if necessary. 🎧 5.6

1. _____ bag (n)   a. to try to win against someone

2. _____ club (n)   b. a person who doesn't win

3. _____ coach (n)   c. a person who is the best or first in a game or sport

4. _____ compete (v)   d. an event where people try to win a prize

5. _____ competition (n)   e. a group of people who do a sport or activity together

6. _____ fit (adj)   f. doing an activity as a job

7. _____ lose (v)   g. to not win

8. _____ loser (n)   h. in good health

9. _____ professional (adj)   i. a person who teaches others to play a sport

10. _____ winner (n)   j. something you use to carry things

B Complete the conversation with the correct form of the words from activity A. Then practice the conversation with a partner.

A: What do you do on the weekends?

B: I'm on a darts team. We play every weekend.

A: I love darts. It's very popular in England. A lot of people play it. My friend is a ¹_____ dart player. He ²_____ around the world. Do you think darts is really a sport?

B: Yes, I think it is. It takes skill to play, and it's physical. I exercise every day to stay ³_____.

A: How is your team? Do you win a lot?

B: Sometimes we win, but we often ⁴_____. It's fun being the ⁵_____, but it's OK being the ⁶_____. Our ⁷_____ wants us to have fun.

A: Do you want to play now?

B: Sure! Hold on. I have some darts in my bag.

C Work with a partner to complete the word form table. Use a dictionary to check your answers.

Verb	Noun	Verb	Noun
1.	coach	5.	competition
win	2.	ride	6.
3.	loser	7.	swimmer
play	4.	dance	8.

REFLECT   Discuss uncommon sports.

You are going to watch a video about an unusual sport. Work in a small group. Look at the infographic. Then discuss the questions.

Uncommon Sports around the World

CHEESE ROLLING
Up to fourteen players roll wheels of cheese down a hill and run after them. The first person to the bottom of the hill is the winner.

UNDERWATER HOCKEY
Two teams play hockey underwater. They compete in a swimming pool. The team with the most goals at the end of the game wins.

CHESS BOXING
Two players play nine minutes of chess. Every three minutes, they stop and box for three minutes. To be the winner, a player needs to win either the chess game or boxing match.

 +

YUKIGASSEN
Two teams compete in a snowball fight. They try to hit each other with snowballs to get players "out." The team with the most players at the end of the game wins.

1. What does this infographic show?
2. Which of these sports are individual sports?
3. Which ones do you think are difficult? Which do you think are fun?
4. Which ones do you want to watch? Which ones do you want to play?

A Scrabble
competition in
Abuja, Nigeria

THE SPORT OF SCRABBLE

A PREVIEW How do activities such as sports and games help people? Brainstorm ideas in a small group. Then share your ideas with the class.

Playing sports helps people stay healthy.

B PHRASES TO KNOW Work with a partner. Discuss the meaning of these phrases from the video. Then take turns answering the questions.

1. What **life lessons** can we learn from sports?

2. What are some ways people **make money** in sports?

C MAIN IDEAS Watch the video. Put the main ideas in the correct order (1–3). ▶ 5.1

_____ Scrabble helps people as a sport.

_____ Scrabble matches the definition of a sport.

_____ Scrabble is an official sport in Nigeria.

D DETAILS Watch the video again. Write T for *True* or F for *False*. ▶ 5.1

1. _____ Scrabble players make words from letters.

2. _____ Good Scrabble players have skills.

3. _____ Scrabble players' brains get exercise during a competition.

4. _____ Scrabble players do not need to be fit.

5. _____ Many people in Nigeria believe Scrabble is a sport.

6. _____ There are not many Scrabble clubs in Nigeria.

7. _____ There are professional Scrabble coaches in Nigeria.

8. _____ Wellington Jighere is a Scrabble World Champion from Nigeria.

9. _____ Jighere believes that Scrabble helps people in many ways.

10. _____ Some people make money playing Scrabble.

E Do you think Scrabble is a sport? Work with a small group and share your ideas. Then share your ideas as a class.

COMMUNICATION TIP

Use these phrases to show you agree or disagree.

Agree	Disagree
I agree.	*I don't agree.*
Me, too.	*I don't think so.*
I think so, too.	*I disagree.*
That's right.	*That's not right.*

Debate if an activity is a sport or not.

To debate is to discuss both sides of a subject. You are going to debate with a partner the question: *Is an activity a sport or not?* One person will say the activity is a sport, and the other person will say it isn't. Use the ideas, vocabulary, and skills from the unit.

F MODEL Listen to two people debate. Complete the chart with one word or a number. 🎧 5.7

Reasons chess is a sport	Reasons chess isn't a sport
There are ¹_____ players and one ²_____.	These reasons are true for ³_____, too.
Players need ⁴_____.	Chess isn't ⁵_____.
Players feel tired after ⁶_____, and that shows they use their bodies.	⁷_____ is not a physical activity.

SPEAKING SKILL   Use listing words and phrases

When you give more than one reason or example, you can use listing words and phrases like these:

First,/My first reason (is)   Next,   One more example (is)
Second,/A second example (is)   Another reason (is)   Finally,/My last reason (is)

*There are many reasons why swimming is my favorite sport. **First,** I love water. **Another reason is** it's good exercise.*

G APPLY Listen again. Check (✓) the words and phrases you hear. 🎧 5.7

☐ First   ☐ A second reason   ☐ Second,   ☐ Another reason   ☐ Finally,

---

GRAMMAR   Conjunctions *and* and *but*

We use *and* and *but* to connect two simple sentences into a compound sentence.

And connects two sentences with similar ideas or adds a new idea.

> *Players use their feet in soccer, **and** they use their heads, too.*

But connects two sentences with different ideas.

> *Baseball is popular in many countries, **but** there are more soccer players around the world.*

H GRAMMAR Complete the sentences with *and* or *but*.

1. Junko hopes she wins the game, _____ her team is not very good.

2. My brother plays many sports, _____ he is good at all of them.

3. Good players are fit, _____ this helps them not get tired.

4. I like to win, _____ I often lose.

5. My friends and I watch sports together, _____ we don't like playing sports.

I GRAMMAR Complete each sentence. Use *and* or *but*.

1. Some people think Scrabble is a sport, _____.

2. Competing is fun, _____.

3. Exercising is imporant, _____.

4. Losing a game isn't fun, _____.

5. Chess boxing is an uncommon sport, _____.

6. All sports have rules, _____.

7. Coaches help players get better, _____.

PRONUNCIATION   Sentence stress: Content words 🎧5.8

In sentences, we stress words with meaning, like nouns and verbs. These are called content words. Content words include the following:

Nouns	Main verbs	Adjectives	Question words	Adverbs	Negatives
sports	play	popular	who	always	isn't
game	compete	fit	what	usually	don't
team	win	healthy	how	never	can't

Remember to stress the strong syllable in a word with more than one syllable.

*My **bro**ther com**petes** in **run**ning and **swim**ming.*

J PRONUNCIATION Listen to the sentences. The circles show the number of stressed syllables. Tap your finger on the **bold** syllables in the content words. Then listen and repeat the sentences. 🎧 5.9

O   O   O   O   O   O   O

1. My **bro**ther **likes hock**ey.

2. The **team u**sually **wins**.

3. I **don't like** to **ex**ercise.

4. **Chess isn't** a **sport**.

5. My **fa**ther **likes watch**ing **sports**.

6. You **use** your **arms** and **legs** in **swim**ming.

7. We **like** to **win**, but **some**times we **lose**.

8. My **aunt likes** Scrab**ble and **chess**.

K PRONUNCIATION Practice the conversation with a partner. Stress the content words.

A: **What sports** do you **like**?

B: **Soc**cer and **base**ball.

A: **Why** do you **like** them?

B: They're **fun** and **phy**sical.

L BRAINSTORM Work with a partner. Choose an activity from the ideas below or your own idea. Brainstorm reasons why it is a sport and reasons why it's not a sport.

e-Gaming	Individual players or teams compete to win a video game.
Fishing	People compete to catch the biggest fish or the most fish.
Competitive eating	People compete to eat the most food in a short time.
Parkour	People move through a place, such as a playground, as fast as they can. They run, jump, swing, roll, etc.

M PLAN Decide who will say your activity is a sport and who will say it isn't. Also, decide who will speak first. Then practice your debate.

N UNIT TASK Debate if your activity is a sport. When you listen to other debates, decide who has the better argument.

REFLECT

A Check (✓) the Reflect activities you can do and the academic skills you can use.

☐ categorize sports

☐ explore opinions about sports

☐ discuss uncommon sports

☐ debate if an activity is a sport or not

☐ listen for opinions

☐ use listing words and phrases

☐ gerunds

☐ conjunctions *and* and *but*

☐ brainstorm

B Check (✓) the vocabulary words from the unit that you know. Circle words you still need to practice. Add any other words that you learned.

NOUN	VERB	ADJECTIVE	ADVERB & OTHER
bag	compete	fit	against
club	lose	physical ^{AW}	
coach	practice	professional ^{AW}	
competition	ride	whole	
loser	win		
player			
rule			
skill			
team ^{AW}			
winner			

C Reflect on the ideas in the unit as you answer these questions.

1. What are some good things about sports?

_____

_____

2. What is the most important thing you learned in this unit?

_____

_____

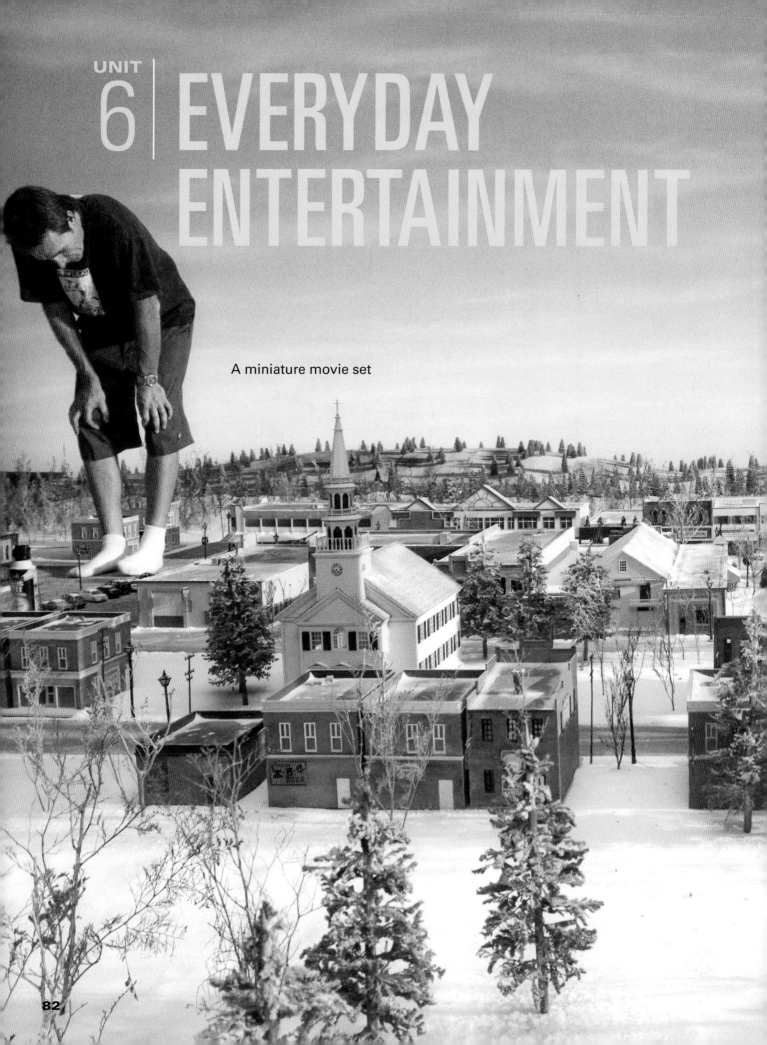

A miniature movie set

IN THIS UNIT

▸ Analyze your entertainment preferences

▸ Discuss connecting to others online

▸ Compare activities you do alone and with others

▸ Give a demonstration

SKILLS

LISTENING
Listen for sequence words

SPEAKING
Check understanding

GRAMMAR
Be going to

Imperatives

CRITICAL THINKING
Analyze information

CONNECT TO THE TOPIC

1. Describe what you see in the photo.
2. What kinds of movies do you like to watch?

83

PREPARE TO LISTEN

A ACTIVATE Work with a partner. Match the words to the images. Then discuss other kinds of entertainment you know.

amusement park	movies	sports	TV
concert	museum	theater	video games

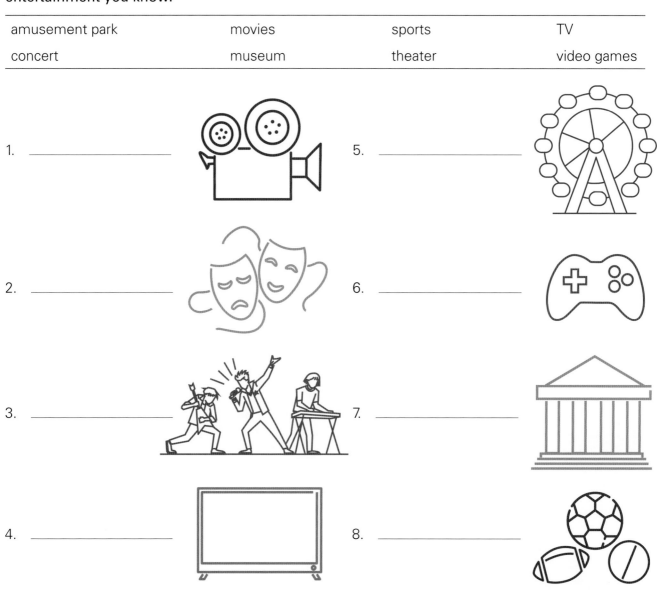

1. _____

2. _____

3. _____

4. _____

5. _____

6. _____

7. _____

8. _____

B VOCABULARY Listen to the words. Complete the conversations with the correct form of the words. Then practice the conversations with a partner. 🎧 6.1

choose (v)	find out (v phr)	laugh (v)	online (adv)	real (adj)
expensive (adj)	free (adj)	mistake (n)	perfect (adj)	website (n)

1. **A:** Who is your favorite movie star?

    B: I don't have a favorite. It's hard to _____ because there are so many good ones.

2. **A:** I want to go to the new amusement park. What do you want to do?

    B: That sounds great. Let's _____ if it's open today.

3. **A:** My friend and I make videos for YouTube. We're not professionals, so the

   videos aren't _____. We make a lot of _____. But

   they are fun to make. We _____ a lot when we make them.

   B: That's OK. People like to see _____ people.

4. **A:** Do you ever go to the movies?

   B: No. Going to a movie is _____, and I don't have a lot of money.

   A: I agree. I usually watch movies at home. It's _____.

5. **A:** I want to share videos _____. Which _____ do

   you use?

   B: I share my videos on YouTube.

CRITICAL THINKING   Analyze information

When you analyze information, you think about it carefully. This helps you
understand better. For example, when you analyze a movie you like, you consider
which parts you like. Perhaps you enjoy the story, or you think the actors are
very good.

REFLECT   Analyze your entertainment preferences.

You are going to hear about a new kind of entertainment. Consider what
kinds of entertainment you like. Read the statements. Write A for *Always*, S
for *Sometimes*, or N for *Never*. Do you like to watch, listen, or look at things
(passive entertainment) or make, play, or do things (active entertainment)?

_____ I watch TV, movies, or videos.   _____ I play video games.

_____ I make videos.   _____ I watch sports.

_____ I listen to music.   _____ I play sports.

_____ I play a musical instrument,   _____ I look at art.
       like the guitar.
                                              _____ I make art.
_____ I watch people play video games
       online.

WHAT'S NEW IN ENTERTAINMENT

Young people act in front of a phone camera in Hyderabad, India.

A PREDICT Look at the photo and read the caption. What type of entertainment do you think the news story is about? Listen to the first part of the story and check your answer. 🎧6.2

    a. Camera apps

    b. Online videos

    c. Reality TV

B PHRASES TO KNOW Work with a partner. Discuss the meaning of these phrases from the news story. Then take turns answering the questions.

    1. TikTok stars make mistakes and can laugh **at themselves**. Can you laugh **at yourself**? Give an example.

    2. There are **tons of** videos online. There are videos for anything you're interested in. Do you have **tons of** anything? What?

C MAIN IDEAS Listen to the whole story and choose the main idea. 🎧6.3

    a. How movie and TV stars are different from YouTube and TikTok stars

    b. What Generation Z people do when they have free time and why

    c. What to do when you have free time on the weekends

D DETAILS Listen to part of the story again. Put the reasons in the order you hear them (1–5). 🎧6.4

    ____ People connect with YouTube and TikTok stars.

    ____ People on YouTube and TikTok are not perfect.

    ____ There are tons of videos.

    ____ YouTube and TikTok are free.

    ____ YouTube and TikTok stars are normal people.

E Discuss the questions in a small group.

    1. What do you know about YouTube and TikTok?

    2. Do you enjoy watching YouTube and TikTok videos?

    3. Can you think of reasons why people like to watch YouTube and TikTok videos?

Sequence words tell the order of events. A speaker uses them to explain how to do something. Listen for these words to help you understand the order of steps or events.

> Buying a movie ticket online is easy. **First,** choose a movie you want to see. **Second,** go online to the movie theater's website. **Third,** click on the time you want to see the movie. **Next,** click on the number of tickets you want to buy. **After (that),** pay the fee. **Then** show your online ticket on your phone at the movie theater. **Finally,** enjoy the movie!

F   APPLY Listen to how to post a YouTube video. Work with a partner and put the sentences in order (1–8). Then listen again and add the correct sequence words to complete the sentences. 🎧 6.5

Order

_____   _____, find a good place to record.

_____   _____, sign in or make an account on YouTube.

_____   _____, plan your video. What do you want to say? Who do you want in your video?

_____   _____, click *publish* and check your video online.

_____   _____, record the video.

_____   _____, tell your friends to watch your video.

_____   _____, practice. Practicing is going to make your video better.

_____   _____ upoad your video, add a title, and describe your video.

GRAMMAR   *Be going to*

We use *be going to* + the base form of a verb to talk about plans in the future. We often pronounce *going to* as *gonna*.

> I **am going to watch** a movie tonight.
> He **is going to make** a YouTube video this weekend.
> They **are going to go** online today.

For negative statements, add *not* between *be* and *going to*.

> We **are not going to stay** home tonight.

We can use the same contractions we use with *be* in the simple present.

> I**'m going to visit** friends this weekend.
> She**'s not going to use** that website./She **isn't going to use** that website.
> They**'re not going to go** to the party./They **aren't going to go** to the party.

G GRAMMAR Complete the conversation with the correct form of *be going to* and the verbs. Use contractions if possible.

A: Hi Talia. What are you going to do this weekend?

B: Hey Franciso. I ¹_____ (see) my family. They

²_____ (visit) me at school this weekend.

A: That's nice! Do you have any plans?

B: We have some plans together, but I ³_____ (not be) with

them all day.

A: Why not?

B: I have two tests on Monday. I ⁴_____ (study). But

first, they ⁵_____ (meet) me at my dorm. Then I

⁶_____ (show) them around the campus. After that, they

⁷_____ (do) things on their own.

A: What are they going to do?

B: My little brother likes soccer, so he ⁸_____ (watch)

the university soccer game. My sister is a college student too, so

she ⁹_____ (go) to the library with me. My parents

¹⁰_____ (visit) the art museum.

A: Are you going to meet up again later?

B: Yes. We ¹¹_____ (have) dinner together this evening,

but they ¹²_____ (not stay) the night.

They ¹³_____ (drive) home.

A: Sounds like a great weekend. Have a good time!

H GRAMMAR Work with a partner. Talk about your plans for this weekend. What are you going to do? What are you not going to to?

REFLECT   Discuss connecting to others online.

Work with a small group. Answer the questions.

1. The news story gives some examples of how people connect with YouTube and TikTok stars. Can you think of other ways online videos connect people?

2. What other ways do people connect online?

3. How is connecting online the same as connecting in real life? How is it different?

PREPARE TO WATCH

A ACTIVATE Listen to the words. Put a check (✓) next to the ones you know. 🎧 6.6

a few (phr)	boring (adj)	excited (adj)	helpful (adj)	motivated (adj)
bored (adj)	date (n)	funny (adj)	interesting (adj)	screen (n)

B VOCABULARY Match the parts of the conversations.

1. _____ YouTube stars are very **motivated**.

2. _____ I'm **bored**. I have nothing to do.

3. _____ I laugh every time I see that movie.

4. _____ I like the size of your phone **screen**.

5. _____ The new movie theater opens today.

6. _____ Why don't you want to go to a museum?

7. _____ I put the **date** on every photo I take.

8. _____ Do you know any YouTube stars?

9. _____ My friend watches videos online for fun.

10. _____ I don't know how to cook.

a. Me, too! Videos look better on it.

b. That's a good idea. I never remember to do that!

c. I don't either, but cooking videos are **helpful**.

d. I don't like them. I think they are **boring**.

e. Yes, but I only like a **few** of them. I follow three of them.

f. Yes, they have many reasons to make videos.

g. Me, too! It's a **funny** movie.

h. I know! I'm **excited** to go there.

i. I do, too. People make a lot of **interesting** videos.

j. I'm going to see a movie. Do you want to come with me?

C PERSONALIZE Take turns asking and answering the questions with a partner.

1. What do you do when you're **bored**?

2. What is something you're **excited** about?

3. What is an **interesting** book or movie? What is a **funny** one?

4. Who do you know that is **helpful**?

Taking a selfie in
Shanghai, China

D Choose the correct word.

1. I don't like this movie. It's **boring / bored**.
2. When I'm **boring / bored**, I watch TV.
3. I like going to concerts. It's **exciting / excited** to listen to music in person.
4. My friends are **exciting / excited** to play the new video game.
5. Let's go to the museum. It's **interesting / interested** to look at art.
6. I am **interesting / interested** in that book. Is it good?
7. Students are **motivating / motivated** to get good grades.
8. This speaker is **motivating / motivated**. I want to do what he says.

REFLECT Compare activities you do alone and with others.

You are going to watch a video about "with me" videos. Think about your
habits. Write A for something you usually do *alone* or W for something you
do *with other people*. Compare your answers with a partner.

_____ buy new clothes   _____ go to the movies

_____ eat dinner at a restaurant   _____ study

_____ exercise   _____ travel

WATCH & SPEAK

WITH ME

A PREDICT What is a "with me" video? Choose the best answer. Then watch the first part of the video and check your answer. ▶ 6.1

    a. In a "with me" video, we watch another person do something.
    b. In a "with me" video, we listen to stories about a person's life.
    c. In a "with me" video, we learn about how different workers do their work.

B PHRASES TO KNOW Choose the best answer to complete each sentence.

    1. If something happens **more and more**, it . . .

        a. decreases (↓).   b. increases (↑).

    2. If something **catches your attention**, it . . .

        a. doesn't interest you.   b. interests you.

C MAIN IDEAS Watch the whole video. Choose the four main ideas. ▶ 6.2

"With me" videos . . .

a. are for people who live alone.
b. are a new kind of video.
c. are popular everywhere.
d. are only popular in some places.
e. show people how to do things.
f. connect people.
g. are a kind of entertainment.

D DETAILS Watch again. Check (✓) the kinds of videos you hear about. ▶ 6.2

☐ clean with me ☐ drive with me ☐ get ready with me
☐ cook with me ☐ eat with me ☐ shop with me
☐ draw with me ☐ exercise with me ☐ study with me

E Discuss the questions in a small group.

1. Do you watch "with me" videos? Why or why not?
2. What kinds of "with me" videos do you think are helpful?
3. What kind of people make "with me" videos?

A woman makes a "with me" video of herself cooking a delicious Asian fusion meal.

Give a demonstration.

You are going to give a demonstration of how to do something. Use the ideas, vocabulary, and skills from the unit.

GRAMMAR Imperatives

We use imperatives to give instructions or explain how to do something. The imperative is the base form of the verb. It does not have a subject. We understand the subject is "You."

Sit down. **Open** your book. **Get** ready.

We often use sequence words with imperatives.

First, **write** your name. Then **wait** for directions.

We use *please* to be more polite. We use *do not/don't* for negatives.

Please **be** quiet. **Don't talk**.

F MODEL Listen to a person explain how to make a photo book. Complete the steps with the imperatives you hear. 🎧6.7

1. First, _____ a folder for every month on your phone.

2. Second, _____ your photos into the folders.

3. Next, _____ the photos you are going to use.

4. Then _____ the photos to a photo book app.

5. After that, _____ the photos in your book online.

6. Finally, _____ the book.

G GRAMMAR Complete the instructions with the imperative. Then put the sentences in the correct order (1 to 6).

Order

____ _____ (wait) 3 minutes and _____ (remove) the tea bag.

____ _____ (fill) a cup with the hot water.

____ _____ (put) a tea bag in the hot water.

____ If you want, _____ (add) sugar or milk to your tea and _____ (stir) it with a spoon.

____ _____ (boil) some water.

____ _____ (drink) your hot cup of tea.

PRONUNCIATION   Reduced structure words 🎧6.8

We often reduce structure words. Structure words include articles (*a, an, the*), prepositions (*in, at, with*), pronouns (*you, she*), helping verbs (*is, do, can*), and conjunctions (*and, but*).

We reduce structure words by changing the vowel sounds to /ə/ or /ɪ/.

Full form	Reduced form	Example
a, the	/ə/, /ðə/	It's a video. The video is good.
and	/ən/, /ɪn/, /n/	Watch and learn.
can	/kən/, /kn/	A video can help. So can a book.
for	/fər/	I need to study for class.
of	/əv/	Have a cup of coffee.
or	/ər/	Do you want coffee or tea?
to	/tə/	I am ready to go.
you	/yə/	How are you?

H PRONUNCIATION Listen and notice the reduced structure words. Then practice the conversation with a partner. 🎧6.9

A: What're your plans <u>for</u> <u>the</u> weekend?

B: I'm not sure.

A: <u>Can</u> <u>you</u> help make <u>a</u> YouTube video?

B: Sure! When?

A: Saturday <u>or</u> Sunday. What's better?

B: Both <u>are</u> OK.

I PRONUNCIATION Listen and write the structure word you hear. 🎧6.10

1. I like _____ book. It's funny _____ interesting.

2. Do _____ like watching movies at home _____ at _____ theater?

3. I like all kinds _____ entertainment.

4. _____ you take this book _____ your roommate?

5. I want _____ visit _____ museum _____ go _____ the park.

6. Let's start _____ book club _____ the students at school.

J APPLY Listen again to someone explain how to make a photo book. Match the instructions to what the speaker says to check that listeners understand. 🎧 6.7

1. ____ Second, put your photos into the folders.

a. Do you have any questions?

2. ____ Then upload the photos to a photo book app.

b. Does that make sense?

3. ____ After that, arrange the photos in your book online.

c. In other words, try putting them in different places on each page.

4. ____ Finally, print the book.

d. What I mean is, look at the dates on the photos and put them in the correct folders.

K PLAN Complete the chart to plan your presentation. Think of something that you know how to do well and the steps to do it.

I know how to . . .	I follow these steps.

L PRACTICE Use your notes from activity K and the model to help you prepare your presentation. Practice giving your presentation to a partner. You can also record yourself and make a "with me" video.

M UNIT TASK Give your demonstration to the class.

REFLECT

A Check (✓) the Reflect activities you can do and the academic skills you can use.

☐ analyze your entertainment preferences

☐ discuss connecting to others online

☐ compare activities you do alone and with others

☐ give a demonstration

☐ listen for sequence words

☐ check understanding

☐ *be going to*

☐ imperatives

☐ analyze information

B Check (✓) the vocabulary words from the unit that you know. Circle words you still need to practice. Add any other words that you learned.

NOUN	VERB	ADJECTIVE	ADVERB & OTHER
date	choose	bored	a few
mistake	find out	boring	online
screen	laugh	excited	
website		expensive	
		free	
		funny	
		helpful	
		interesting	
		motivated ᴬᵂ	
		perfect	
		real	

C Reflect on the ideas in the unit as you answer these questions.

1. What do you think about online videos now?

_____

_____

2. What is the most important thing you learned in this unit?

_____

_____

7 DO WHAT YOU LOVE

Street performers at a festival in the United States

CONNECT TO THE TOPIC

1. Does this kind of work look fun?

2. How do people find jobs?

PREPARE TO LISTEN

A ACTIVATE Write a list of jobs you know on a separate piece of paper. Share your list with a partner. Then discuss jobs that have things in common.

Doctors, nurses, and dentists care for people.

B VOCABULARY Listen to the words. Complete the sentences with the correct form of the words. 🔊7.1

advice (n)	especially (adv)	get better (v phr)	prefer (v)	suggest (v)
be good at (v phr)	exciting (adj)	possible (adj)	situation (n)	well (adv)

1. I don't want a boring job. I want to be a firefighter. That is _____ work.

2. My work _____ is difficult. I work many hours a day and on weekends, too.

3. I want to be a nurse. My teacher _____ that I talk to a nurse about her job.

4. Martha _____ teaching. Her students are happy and learn a lot.

5. It's difficult to go to school and have a job, but it is _____ to do both if you work hard.

6. I like everything about my job, _____ the people I work with.

7. I _____ studying at night. It's quiet then.

8. Eduardo does _____ in his art classes. His drawings are really good.

9. When I have a big problem, I ask my parents for _____.

10. I take good pictures, but I want to _____. I want to be great.

C PERSONALIZE Discuss the questions in a small group.

1. What **advice** do you have for students taking this class next year? **Suggest** two things.
2. What is something you are **especially** happy about right now?
3. What is a **situation** that you hope **gets better**?

D Listen and complete the sentences with the words you hear. 🔊7.2

Juan: I am a salesperson. I sell computers. I ¹_____ talking to people. I talk to people in any ²_____. I ³_____ a job with people.

Li: I am a nurse. I like helping sick people. I ⁴_____ like helping children. I like seeing them ⁵_____ and go home.

Engineers test a robot at Northeastern University in Boston, Massachusetts, USA.

Omar: I am a student. I do ⁶_____ in my science and math classes. My father is an engineer, so it's ⁷_____ I will be an engineer, too. My teacher gives me ⁸_____. She ⁹_____ that I do what makes me happy.

Discuss jobs.

You are going to hear a conversation about choosing jobs. Discuss these questions with a partner.

1. What is a boring job?
2. What is an exciting job?
3. What is something you are good at?
4. What is a possible job for you?

THE JOB FOR ME

A sports medicine student at Humboldt University in Berlin, Germany, studies muscle activity.

A PREVIEW Look at the photo and read the caption. What is the man on the computer doing? Discuss with a partner.

B PREDICT You will hear a conversation between a student and an academic advisor. What kinds of things do academic advisors talk about with students?

C MAIN IDEAS Listen to the conversation. Choose the correct answers. 🎧 7.3

1. What does Peter have questions about?

   a. Biology

   b. His future

   c. Physical therapy

2. What three things does the academic advisor say are important when thinking about a job?

   a. How you like to work

   b. If you like school

   c. If you like sports

   d. What you enjoy

   e. What you're good at

LISTENING SKILL Take notes in a T-chart

One way to take notes is with a T-chart. A T-chart separates information into two categories, like questions and answers. Write the questions on the left and the answers on the right. Don't write every word. Write words that will help you remember the information later.

Questions	Answers
Favorite class?	*English*
Study alone or with others?	*alone*
Free time?	*run*

D DETAILS Listen to part of the conversation again. Take notes on Peter's answers. 🎧 7.4

Questions	Answers
What classes are you doing well in?	1. _____
What classes do you like?	2. _____
What makes you happy outside of school?	3. _____
How do you like to work?	4. _____

CRITICAL THINKING   Ask questions

Asking questions helps us learn more about a topic. *What, Why,* and *How* questions are especially helpful.

> **What** *skills do I need for this job?*
> **Why** *are these skills important?*
> **How** *can I learn more about the job?*

E APPLY Work with a small group. Which of the academic advisor's questions in the conversation do you think is most helpful? What other questions do you think are important to think about when looking for a job?

GRAMMAR   *Would like*

We use *would like* to talk about what we want now and in the future. *Would like* is followed by a noun or the infinitive (*to* + verb).

> *I* **would like** *your advice. I'**d like** to talk to you about my future.*
> *He* **would like** *to work in an office. He'**d like** a big window.*
> *They* **would like** *to take pre-med classes. They'**d like** to become doctors.*

We use *would not* or *wouldn't* for negatives.

> *She* **would not like** *to work from home. She* **wouldn't like** *to be alone all day.*

For questions, put *would* before the subject.

> **Would you like** *to talk with my sister?*
> *What kind of work situation* **would you like***?*

F GRAMMAR Write the words in the correct order to make sentences or questions.

1. like / would / to / teach / they

   _____

2. a sales job / I / like / would / not

   _____

3. she / with children / work / to / like / would / ?

   _____

4. like / class / wouldn't / he / the

   _____

5. you / would / what / skills / like / ?

   _____

Working from home

G GRAMMAR Listen to a student talk about what he would like to be. Answer the questions with complete sentences. 🎧 7.5

1. What would Pedro like to be?

   _____

2. Why would he like to do this?

   _____

3. What would he like to get better at?

   _____

4. Who would he like to talk to?

   _____

5. When would he like to have this job?

   _____

H GRAMMAR Discuss the questions with a partner.

1. Where would you like to live?
2. Would you like to work for the same company your whole life?
3. Would you like to make a lot of money or have a job you love?
4. What would you like to learn more about?

REFLECT Discuss what's important at work.

Look at the list of what people think is important in a job. Add your own ideas. Then check (✓) the three most important things for you. Compare your answers with a partner.

☐ being happy   ☐ the people you work with

☐ the company you work for   ☐ the skills needed

☐ how interesting the work is   ☐ where you work

☐ how much money you make   ☐ _____

☐ the number of hours   ☐ _____

PREPARE TO WATCH

A **ACTIVATE** Listen to the words. Put a check (✓) next to the ones you know. 🎧 7.6

actually (adv)	career (n)	expert (n)	mean (v)	save (v)
(be) willing (v phr)	discover (v)	location (n)	office (n)	time (n)

B **VOCABULARY** Read the sentences. Choose the words with the same meaning as the words in bold.

1. Many people don't like their jobs, but I **actually** love mine!

   a. really   b. instead   c. too

2. I **am willing** to try new things. I think it's fun!

   a. am happy   b. am OK   c. am unhappy

3. I would like a **career** in business after college.

   a. class   b. degree   c. job

4. Many people **discover** jobs online. Many companies post jobs on their websites.

   a. ask about   b. do   c. find

5. Talia knows a lot about computers. She is an **expert**.

   a. person who knows a lot   b. person who sells things   c. person who teaches

6. What is the **location** of your school?

   a. home   b. place   c. website

7. *Easy* **means** "not hard."

   a. equals (=)   b. does not equal   c. makes

National Geographic Explorer
Dr. Albert Lin at work in Mongolia

8. The **office** is closed. Everyone is working from home.

   a. classroom   b. library   c. workplace

9. Panda bears are my favorite animal. They are in danger. I would like to **save** the pandas.

   a. check   b. help   c. track

10. We walk to school three **times** a week—on Mondays, Wednesdays, and Fridays.

    a. hours   b. minutes   c. occasions; moments

C Listen and complete the paragraph with the words you hear. 🎧 7.7

Who is an explorer? Someone from the past, like Christopher Columbus or Ibn Battuta? A scientific

¹_____? ²_____, there are many National Geographic Explorers doing

important work today. Some Explorers have ³_____ in science, but not all of them.

They have other jobs, too. They work in different ⁴_____, from ⁵_____ to

oceans, but they all want the same thing: to ⁶_____ our planet. They bring attention to a

lot of important things because they ⁷_____ to ask questions. A lot of

⁸_____, that ⁹_____ they ¹⁰_____ new things, too.

REFLECT   Identify skills you have.

You are going to watch a video about an explorer with special job skills. Work with a partner.
For each category of skill, give an example of something you can do. Start with "I can..."

Computer skills   Physical skills (exercise, sports, etc.)

Language skills   Technical skills (cooking, building, fixing, etc.)

People skills (communication)

A diver uses a metal detector in Oman.

DAVID MEARNS: SHIPWRECK HUNTER

A PREVIEW Look at the title of the video, the photo, and the caption. A *shipwreck hunter* looks for ships underwater and discovers things. With a partner, brainstorm the skills you think a shipwreck hunter needs.

B PHRASES TO KNOW Work with a partner. Discuss the meaning of these phrases from the video. Then take turns answering the questions.

1. Aya **sort of** wants to be a teacher and **sort of** wants to be a doctor. What is something you **sort of** want to do?

2. Juan loves the ocean. He is **dying to** go to the beach this weekend. What are you **dying to** do?

C MAIN IDEAS Watch the video. Then choose another title for it. ▶ 7.1

a. Working with Sea Animals

b. A Career Underwater

c. Career Advice

d. Exciting Jobs on Land

D DETAILS Watch the video again. Choose the correct answers. ▶ 7.1

1. People **are / are not** surprised when they hear about David Mearns's job.

2. Mearns works **alone / with a team**.

3. Mearns dives **4 / 25** times a day.

4. They are underwater for over **100 / 1,000** hours.

5. Mearns **loves / hates** his job.

6. Shipwreck hunters are dying to get to work because there is going to be a new **discovery / problem** every day.

7. **One / The only** skill a shipwreck hunter needs is diving.

8. They bring in **teachers / experts** who can look at what they discover.

> **COMMUNICATION TIP**
>
> When you don't hear or understand someone, use these expressions to ask the speaker to repeat.
>
> *Who? What? When?*
>
> *Can you repeat that (please)?*
>
> *Can you say that again?*
>
> *What was that?*

E Read the Communication Tip. Listen to a conversation. Check (✓) the expressions you hear. 🎧 7.8

☐ Can you repeat that?   ☐ What?   ☐ When?

☐ Can you say that again?   ☐ What was that?   ☐ Who?

Describe your dream job.

You are going to give a presentation about your dream job. Use the ideas, vocabulary, and skills from the unit.

SPEAKING SKILL   Describe with details

When we describe a situation, we "paint a picture" of it with our words. We talk about actions and use adjectives to say how things look, sound, smell, taste, and feel. Describing a situation in detail helps your listeners "see" it in their mind.

F MODEL Listen to a person describe her dream job. Check (✓) the details you hear. 🔊 7.9

Actions	☐ drinking coffee	☐ sitting at a desk	☐ talking to people
	☐ finding mistakes	☐ suggesting ideas	☐ using the computer
	☐ reading a new book	☐ taking notes	☐ writing a book
Adjectives	☐ big	☐ exciting	☐ peaceful
	☐ boring	☐ famous	☐ quiet
	☐ comfortable	☐ new	☐ small

GRAMMAR   Present continuous

We use the present continuous to talk about things that are happening now. Use *am, is, are* (*not*) + the *-ing* form of the verb.

> I **am talking** on the phone now. I**'m not working**.
> You **are studying** English. You**'re not studying** Chinese.
> Peter **is doing** well in his science class. He **isn't doing** well in his history class.

We can use the same contractions we use with *be* in the simple present.

G GRAMMAR Complete the sentences with the present continuous form of the verbs.

1. Mattias _____ (take) five classes.

2. Jonas and I _____ (walk) to our job right now.

3. Keiko and Jun _____ (meet, not) at the library. They

   _____ (study) in the office.

4. I _____ (read) about careers in the future.

5. My friend works a lot. She _____ (relax) now.

6. Jin _____ (do, not) well at work.

7. Aliya and I _____ (talk) about our dream jobs.

8. I _____ (think, not) about a career in computers.

H GRAMMAR Work with a partner. For each situation, think of three things the people are doing now. Add one more interesting situation of your own. Then share your ideas with the class.

1. I am a teacher.
2. Henry and James are students.
3. David Mearns is a shipwreck hunter.
4. Other: _____

I'm a teacher. I am writing on the board. I'm explaining the grammar. I'm answering students' questions.

PRONUNCIATION Connected speech 🔊7.10

We often connect, or link, words when we're speaking. One way we link words is to connect a final consonant sound to a beginning vowel sound. The final consonant sound becomes the beginning of the next word.

*Do something you're **good at**. Do something you're **goo dat**.*

I PRONUNCIATION Draw lines to link the connected speech in the sentences. Then listen and repeat the sentences. 🔊7.11

1. She needs a job near a bus stop.
2. Sports are a possible career for him.
3. I'd like to suggest a career in medicine.
4. She likes being part of a team.
5. I'm a student. I'm studying to be an engineer.

J PRONUNCIATION Complete the conversation with the words you hear.
Practice the conversation with a partner. 🎧 7.12

good advice	kind of	teaches 8th
in education	loves it	

A: What ¹_____ job do you want?

B: I would like a career ²_____.

A: Do you want to talk to my mother? She ³_____ grade,
and she ⁴_____.

B: Thank you. I would love to talk to her. I'm sure she can give me
⁵_____.

K PLAN Complete the chart with information about your dream job.

What job would you like?	
Where are you?	
What are you doing?	
What would you like to do as part of your job?	
What skills do you need?	

L PRACTICE Use your notes from activity K to prepare your presentation.
Practice giving your presentation to a partner.

M UNIT TASK Present your dream job to the class.

REFLECT

A Check (✓) the Reflect activities you can do and the academic skills you can use.

☐ discuss jobs

☐ discuss what's important at work

☐ identify skills you have

☐ describe your dream job

☐ take notes in a T-chart

☐ describe with details

☐ *would like*

☐ present continuous

☐ ask questions

B Check (✓) the vocabulary words from the unit that you know. Circle words you still need to practice. Add any other words that you learned.

NOUN	VERB	ADJECTIVE	ADVERB & OTHER
advice	be good at	exciting	actually
career	be willing	possible	especially
expert AW	discover		well
location AW	get better		
office	mean		
situation	prefer		
time	save		
	suggest		

C Reflect on the ideas in the unit as you answer these questions.

1. Does anyone in your class have the same dream job? What are some popular dream jobs?

_____

_____

2. What is the most important thing you learned in this unit?

_____

_____

UNIT 8

BIG EFFECTS

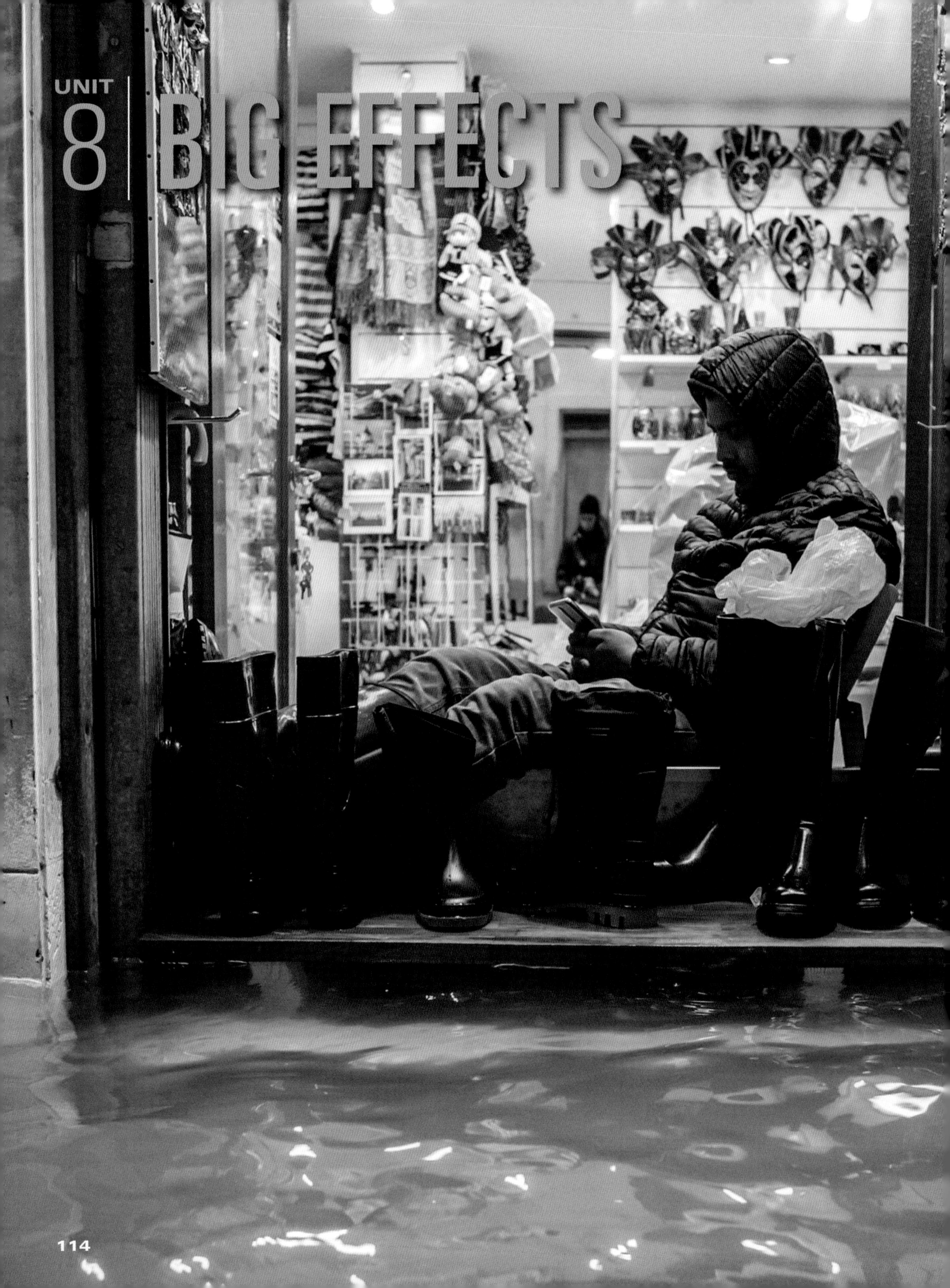

Flooding in Venice, Italy, is not new. But more flooding and higher water levels are damaging the city.

CONNECT TO THE TOPIC

1. How do you think the man feels? Why?
2. How do you feel about changes in the environment?

PREPARE TO LISTEN

A VOCABULARY Listen to the words. Complete the sentences with the correct form of the words. 🎧 8.1

able (adj)	demand (v)	kid (n)	ocean (n)	worried (adj)
amazing (adj)	environment (n)	meeting (n)	trash (n)	young (adj)

1. There are many problems with the _____, such as air pollution. Some places have dirty air.

2. Many people are _____ about global warming.

3. Our planet is _____. There are so many things you see and say, "Wow!"

4. There are over 1.8 billion _____ people, 10–24 years old, in the world.

5. I have a _____ with my boss today. It's from 1–2 p.m.

6. The workers _____ more money because their jobs are difficult.

7. There are five _____ in the world, and the biggest one is the Pacific.

8. When you're a _____, people always ask, "What do you want to be when you grow up?"

9. Every month, my neighborhood has a clean-up day. We pick up a lot of _____.

10. We need people to help with activities for Earth Day. What are you _____ to do?

B PERSONALIZE Discuss the questions in a small group.

1. What is good about being **young**?
2. What is difficult about being **young**?
3. What is something you are **worried** about?
4. What is an example of an **amazing** place?
5. What are you **able** to do now that you were not **able** to do five years ago?
6. When you were a **kid**, what did you want to be?

C Listen to a conversation. Then complete the description with words from activity A. 🎧 8.2

The Green Club is a group of people, ¹_____ and old, that wants to help the environment. They do things like pick up ²_____ and write letters to ³_____ changes in the city. They want ⁴_____ today to have a clean and healthy environment in the future.

REFLECT   Discuss environmental problems.

You are going to listen to a talk about young people helping with environmental problems. Work with a small group. Match the environmental problem to the photo. Then discuss why these are problems.

  a. air pollution

  b. deforestation (cutting down trees)

  c. ocean levels rising (getting higher)

  d. too much trash

1. _____

3. _____

2. _____

4. _____

LISTEN & SPEAK

MAKING A DIFFERENCE NOW

Delaney Reynolds shows
how much the sea will
rise in her lifetime in
Florida, USA.

A PREVIEW Work with a partner. Discuss different ways to help the environment.

One way to help the environment is to use less plastic.

B PHRASES TO KNOW Choose the correct meaning for the phrases from the talk.

1. Another way to help is to **speak out**.

    talk outside / tell people about a problem

2. There are so many ways to **make a difference**.

    be different / do something important

C MAIN IDEAS Listen to the talk and complete the sentences with one to four words. 🔊 8.3

1. One way to help the environment is to _____.

2. A second way is to _____.

3. A third way is to _____.

4. A fourth way is to _____.

D MAIN IDEAS Listen again. Write the way to help (1–4) from activity C next to the person who does it. 🔊 8.3

_____ Delaney Reynolds   _____ Ghislain Irakoze

_____ Felix Finkbeiner   _____ Greta Thunberg

LISTENING SKILL   Listen for numbers and years

Listen for two things to hear the difference between numbers that end in *-teen* and *-ty*: syllable stress and the *t* in the final syllable. When the final syllable is not stressed, the *t* often sounds like a *d*.

thir**teen**	**thir**ty
four**teen**	**for**ty
nine**teen**	**nine**ty

Listen for these different ways to say years.

1990   nineteen ninety
2021   two thousand twenty-one OR two thousand and twenty-one OR
       twenty twenty-one

Use these abbreviations to note numbers: K (thousand), M (million),
B (billion), T (trillion).

E APPLY Listen again. Complete the sentences with a number or year. 🎧 8.3

1. Delaney Reynolds was _____ when she learned about climate change. She is _____ now.

2. In _____, Greta Thunberg did the first school walkout for climate change. She was _____ years old.

3. In _____, Finkbeiner started the Plant-for-the-Planet project. He was _____ years old.

4. Over the years, Plant-for-the-Planet planted over _____ trees in _____ countries.

5. When Ghislain was _____ years old, he learned there were _____ tons of electronic trash every year.

GRAMMAR Simple past of *be*

We use the simple past of *be* to describe things in the past.

> Felix **was** young at the beginning of his Plant-for-the-Planet project. He **was not** even 10 years old. We **were** all excited to learn about these amazing kids.

Add *not* to make a negative statement. The contraction for *was not* is *wasn't*. The contraction for *were not* is *weren't*.

Subject	Verb
I/He/She/It	**was** young/**was not (wasn't)** old.
You/We/They	**were** young/**were not (weren't)** old.

F GRAMMAR Complete the sentences with the correct form of the simple past of *be*. Use contractions when possible.

Last summer, my friends and I ¹_____ in Costa Rica, but we
²_____ there on vacation. We ³_____ part of a wildlife
club. The club has different teams that people can choose. I ⁴_____
interested in deforestation, so I ⁵_____ on the tree team. Martina loves
animals, so she ⁶_____ on the animal team. Lucia ⁷_____
sad to hear about the trash in the rivers, so she ⁸_____ on the river
team. I believe we ⁹_____ helpful to our teams. It ¹⁰_____
an amazing trip! When it ¹¹_____ time to leave, I ¹²_____
ready to go home! I wanted to stay longer.

G GRAMMAR Answer the questions with a small group.

1. Where were you yesterday?
2. What was in the news last year?
3. Who was famous five years ago?
4. What were you interested in when you were 13?

REFLECT Analyze ways you help the environment.

Work in a small group. Look at the infographic. Then discuss the questions.

1. What does the infographic show?
2. Which of these activities do you do well?
3. Which can you do better?
4. What other things do you do at home to help the environment? Make your own infographic.

Five Things You Can Do at Home to Help the Environment

1. Recycle.
2. Use less paper.
3. Don't use plastic bags.
4. Use natural products to clean.
5. Don't waste food.

PREPARE TO WATCH

A VOCABULARY Listen to the words in **bold**. Choose the sentence that explains the word in **bold**. 🎧 8.4

1. The students **behave** in class. It is nice to teach them.
   a. The students are good in class.
   b. The students are not good in class.

2. **Earth** is everyone's home. That's why we need to help the environment.
   a. Earth is a place people go to on vacation.
   b. Earth is the third planet from the sun.

3. The weather has an **effect** on people. It can make them happy or sad.
   a. The weather changes people.
   b. The weather doesn't matter to people.

4. It's great you are able to talk **in front of** a group.
   a. You are good at working in a group.
   b. You can talk when a lot of people are looking at you.

5. Please **invite** your friends to the meeting.
   a. Your friends can come to the meeting.
   b. Your friends can't come to the meeting.

6. The **leader** of the United States is the president.
   a. She is a regular member of a group or country.
   b. She controls a group or country.

7. **Make sure** you do the walkout on Friday. It's very important.
   a. Yes, definitely do the walkout.
   b. I'm not sure. Maybe do the walkout.

8. Sometimes things don't work in my house, but then my father **repairs** them.
   a. My father makes things better.
   b. My father makes problems.

9. There are **several** oceans in the world.
   a. There are many oceans in the world.
   b. There are more than two but not many oceans in the world.

10. Diane is a **teenager**.
   a. Diane is between 13 and 19 years old.
   b. Diane is between 20 and 29 years old.

Wildfires of 2020 made the sky orange
in San Francisco, California, USA.

B PERSONALIZE Ask and answer the questions with a partner.

1. How do you feel when you speak **in front of** a large group?
2. What things do you **invite** people to?
3. Do you think you're a good **leader**?
4. What is a good way to **make sure** you remember new words?

REFLECT   Discuss your experience with climate change.

You are going to watch a video about a woman's fight to stop climate change. Climate change is a change in the average conditions—such as temperature and rainfall—in a place over a long period of time. In a small group, discuss the questions.

1. What are some of the effects of climate change?
2. What places in the world have problems because of climate change?
3. What animals have problems because of climate change?

SEVERN **SPOKE** OUT **FIRST**

Filmmaker, writer, and climate change activist Severn Cullis-Suzuki

A PREVIEW Look at the photo, caption, and title. What do you think "Severn Spoke Out First" means?

B MAIN IDEAS Watch the video. Choose the three main ideas. ▶ 8.1

a. Severn was a young member of the United Nations.

b. Severn demanded that world leaders repair the environment.

c. Severn's parents taught her to love Earth.

d. Severn wanted to help the environment.

e. Severn stopped trying to help because no one listened.

C DETAILS Watch again. Complete the sentences with one word or number. ▶ 8.1

1. In _____, Severn gave a speech at a meeting of the United Nations in Brazil.

2. She was _____ years old when she gave her speech.

3. Her speech was _____ minutes.

4. Her parents had a big _____ on her. They are environmentalists.

5. At _____ years old, she started the Environmental Children's Organization (ECO).

6. _____ years later, she was at the meeting of the United Nations in Brazil.

7. _____ members of ECO went with her.

8. The effect of her speech was _____.

9. Severn was a part of many projects as a child, _____, and adult.

CRITICAL THINKING **Understand metaphors**

A metaphor compares two things that aren't the same. When we use a metaphor, we say one thing *is* another thing. We use metaphors to help us understand an idea better.

Earth is everyone's home.

D APPLY Work with a partner. Match the beginning of each metaphor to the end. Discuss what they mean. Then think of your own metaphors for things in the environment.

1. _____ Earth is

2. _____ Trees are

3. _____ The feel of the sun is

4. _____ The ocean is

a. a warm blanket.

b. an underwater world.

c. our lungs.

d. our mother.

You are going to give a presentation about a person who had an effect on your life. Use the ideas, vocabulary, and skills from the unit.

SPEAKING SKILL   Close a presentation

At the end of a presentation or speech, it's good to tell your listeners that your presentation is ending. This helps people listen closely for your final ideas. Use these phrases.

In conclusion, . . .
To conclude, . . .
To close, . . .

E MODEL Listen to someone talk about an important person. What concluding phrase does he use? 🎧 8.5

a. In conclusion
b. To conclude
c. To close

GRAMMAR   Simple past

We use the simple past to talk about completed actions in the past.

> I **learned** about Severn Cullis-Suzuki in class. Leaders of the United Nations **invited** her to speak at a big meeting. She **did not talk** for very long, but everyone **loved** her speech.

We add -ed or -d to the end of verbs to form the simple past. All subjects use the same form.

Subject	Verb
I/You/He/She/It/We/They	**learned/invited/talked/loved**

Use *did not* or *didn't* before the base form of the verb to form the negative.

Subject	Verb
I/You/He/She/It/We/They	**did not (didn't) learn/invite/talk/love**

There are many irregular simple past tense verbs.

be → was/were	give → gave	meet → met	take → took
come → came	go → went	see → saw	teach → taught
do → did	have → had	speak → spoke	tell → told
get → got	make → made	stand → stood	write → wrote

F GRAMMAR Listen again. Complete the sentences with the simple past verbs you hear. 🎧 8.5

My neighbor Mr. Cardenas ¹_____ a big effect on my life. Mr. Cardenas ²_____ like a grandfather to me. We ³_____ very close. I ⁴_____ to his house every Saturday morning during the spring and summer and ⁵_____ him with his garden. He ⁶_____ a big garden with over 40 kinds of flowers. He ⁷_____ me all the plant names and ⁸_____ to me about my life. To close, I want to say that Mr. Cardenas ⁹_____ me how to be kind to people and the environment.

PRONUNCIATION   The focus word 🎧 8.6

In sentences, we usually stress one word more than others. This word is the focus word. The focus word is usually the last content word in a sentence.

*Severn's parents had a big **effect** on her. She demanded help for the **environment**.*

G PRONUNCIATION Underline the focus word in each sentence. Then listen and check your answers. 🎧 8.7

1. She is an amazing teenager.
2. The environment has many problems.
3. We are worried about it.
4. Severn's speech was only six minutes.
5. YouTube has a video of it.
6. My teacher had a big effect on me.

A teacher wins an educator award in California, USA.

H PLAN Answer the questions. Use complete sentences.

1. Who had a big effect on you?

   _____

2. How did you meet this person?

   _____

3. What things did you do together?

   _____

4. What did you learn from this person?

   _____

5. How did this person have a big effect on your life?

   _____

I PRACTICE Review your answers to activity H. Think about what else you want to say about the person who had a big effect on your life. Decide where to add any new ideas. Then practice your presentation.

J UNIT TASK Give your presentation. Bring a picture to show to the class.

An Emirati boy shows his respect by kissing his grandfather's head.

REFLECT

A Check (✓) the Reflect activities you can do and the academic skills you can use.

☐ discuss environmental problems

☐ analyze ways you help the environment

☐ discuss your experience with climate change

☐ give a presentation about an important person

☐ listen for numbers and years

☐ close a presentation

☐ simple past of *be*

☐ simple past

☐ understand metaphors

B Check (✓) the vocabulary words from the unit that you know. Circle words you still need to practice. Add any other words that you learned.

NOUN	VERB	ADJECTIVE	ADVERB & OTHER
Earth	behave	able	in front of
effect	demand	amazing	several
environment ᴬᵂ	invite	worried	
kid	make sure	young	
leader	repair		
meeting			
ocean			
teenager			
trash			

C Reflect on the ideas in the unit as you answer these questions.

1. What can you do to have a good effect on someone?

_____

_____

2. What is the most important thing you learned in this unit?

_____

_____

Using a dictionary Parts of speech

Some words can have more than one part of speech. You can use a dictionary to find the part of speech for a word. A dictionary often uses abbreviations to show the part of speech.

adj—adjective (e.g., *wrong*)   **prep**—preposition (e.g., *on*)
n—noun (e.g., *goal*)   **pron**—pronoun (e.g., *you*)
adv—adverb (e.g., *far*)   **v**—verb (e.g., *believe*)

A Use a dictionary. Write the part of speech for the bold words.

1. **She** is a student. _____

2. It's my **last** day in this class. _____

3. You have a nice **smile**. _____

4. It's good to **meet** you. _____

5. We don't study **at** home. We study in a cafe. _____

6. The cafe is **usually** quieter than the library. _____

Collocations The verb *be*

Collocations are two or more words that often go together. Try to learn a collocation in the same way you learn an individual word. Here are some common collocations with the verb *be*.

be (a number) **years old**   **be good at** (something)
be called (a name)   **be happy to** (do something)
be friends with (someone)   **be interested in** (something)

B Complete the paragraph. Use a collocation from the box above with the correct form of *be*. One collocation is extra.

Hello. I'm Salina. I'm from Chile, but I live in Puente Alto. I [1]_____

25 _____ I have two brothers and one sister. My sister [2]_____

Thelma. I [3]_____ computers, and I [4]_____ computer programming.

I [5]_____ Kareem. We play video games in our free time.

Prefix *un-*

A prefix is a small group of letters. It comes at the beginning of a word. The prefix *un-* means "not."
You can add a prefix to some adjectives to make a word with the opposite meaning.

   un + *comfortable* = ***uncomfortable***, or "not comfortable"

A Choose an adjective to complete each sentence about you.

1. My bedroom is **tidy** / **untidy**.

2. I am **happy** / **unhappy** in my home.

3. My city is **safe** / **unsafe**.

4. I think my home is very **comfortable** / **uncomfortable**.

5. My neighbors are **friendly** / **unfriendly**.

Phrasal verbs With *move*

A phrasal verb is a two- or three- word phrase. It has one verb and another small word. Phrasal verbs
have special meanings. Learn phrasal verbs the way you learn individual words. Here are some
common phrasal verbs with the verb *move*.

move around: to move a lot of times or places   **move over:** to change to the side
move in: to start living in a new home   **move up:** to get a better job
move out: to leave a home forever

B Complete the conversation with words from the box. One word is extra.

around in	out	over	up

A: I found a new apartment! I move [1]_____ next week.

B: I thought you liked your old apartment. Why are you moving [2]_____?

A: I want a place of my own.

B: You're always moving [3]_____!

A: I know. This will be my third apartment this year!

B: Are you staying in the city?

A: Yes. I'm moving [4]_____ to a better job, so I'm getting a nicer apartment!

Using a dictionary Order of definitions

Many words have more than one meaning. In a dictionary, the first definition is the most common meaning, the second definition is the next most-common, and so on. For example, the most common meaning of water is "a colorless liquid made of hydrogen and oxygen."

water (n) **1** a colorless liquid made of hydrogen and oxygen; **2** any body of water, such as a lake; **3** the sea near a country

A Use a dictionary. Write the correct definition for the bold words. Circle the definition number.

1. Businesses **send** emails to customers.

   Meaning: _____

   Definition number: 1 / 2 / 3 / 4

2. I always **check** my homework for errors.

   Meaning: _____

   Definition number: 1 / 2 / 3 / 4

3. I usually **get** lots of calls on my phone.

   Meaning: _____

   Definition number: 1 / 2 / 3 / 4

4. I sometimes **play** sports on the weekend.

   Meaning: _____

   Definition number: 1 / 2 / 3 / 4

Collocations The verb *get*

Remember: Collocations are two or more words that often go together. Try to learn a collocation in the same way you learn an individual word. Here are some common collocations with the verb *get*.

get a job	**get ready**
get dressed	**get together**
get hungry	**get to work**

B Choose the correct collocation to complete each sentence.

1. It takes me an hour to get **ready** / **together** for work.

2. I usually get **a job** / **to work** at 8:30 every morning.

3. I sometimes get **ready** / **hungry** right after lunch.

4. I get **together** / **dressed** with my friends every Thursday evening.

5. I want to get **a job** / **together** in a technology company.

Multiple-meaning words

Some words have two or more different meanings. Sometimes the meanings are similar but not exactly the same.

> The **head** of a restaurant is called a chef. (the person in charge)
> Your **head** includes your brain, eyes, and ears. (the body part on top of your neck)

Use context clues—the words before and after a word—to help you decide which is the correct meaning.

A Choose the correct meaning of the words in bold. Use context clues to help. Check your answers in a dictionary.

1. Curry, a spicy **dish** served with rice, is delicious. — a. a plate or bowl — b. a type of food

2. Your baby is beautiful! He's so **sweet**. — a. easy to love — b. tasting like sugar

3. In many homes, the kitchen **connects** to the living room — a. to join together — b. to like and understand someone

4. The restaurant was old and **sad**. I didn't want to eat there. — a. not happy — b. making you feel unhappy

5. An apple pie **takes** about an hour to cook. — a. to bring with you — b. to need time

Making adjectives stronger or weaker

You can use words like *very* and *really* to make adjectives stronger or weaker. These words are called adverbs of degree.

not very	**kind of**	**pretty**	**really, very**
WEAKER			STRONGER

> This tea is **not very** sweet. It needs sugar.

B Complete the conversations with the phrases in the box.

kind of unhealthy	pretty bad	really salty
not very hungry	pretty big	very good

1. A: This food tastes _____. I don't like it at all!

   B: Really? The food here is usually _____.

2. A: I love _____ foods.

   B: Really? That's _____.

3. A: Do you usually eat breakfast?

   B: No, I'm usually _____ in the morning. What about you? Do you?

   B: No, but I always have a _____ lunch.

Suffixes -er and -or

A suffix is a small group of letters. It comes at the end of a word. The suffixes -er and -or mean "a person or thing that does something." You can add them to some verbs to make nouns.

VERB + -ER = NOUN
play + **er** = **player** or "someone who plays a game."

For one-syllable words that end in a consonant, double the consonant before -er and -or. If a verb ends in –e, remove the final -e. Look in a dictionary to check for the correct spelling.

> hit + **er** = **hitter**, or "someone who hits the ball"
> ride + **er** = **rider**, or "some who rides a bike or horse"

A Complete the sentences with the correct form of the words in the box. One word is extra.

compose	farm	instruct	manage	play	visit	win

1. Someone who runs a business is a(n) _____.

2. Someone who grows fruits and vegetables is a(n) _____.

3. Someone who writes music is called a(n) _____.

4. Someone who goes to a tourist attraction is a(n) _____.

5. Someone who teaches in a college is a(n) _____.

6. Someone who finishes a race first is a(n) _____.

Word forms Nouns and verbs with the same spelling

Some words can be both nouns and verbs, and their spelling does not change.

> V   N
> I **work** at a supermarket. It's hard **work**.

If the word follows an adjective it is more likely to be a noun.

B Read the sentences. Write *N* for *Noun* or *V* for *Verb* for each word in **bold**.

1. _____ I **coach** a soccer team.

2. _____ There's a short **practice** twice a week.

3. _____ I **exercise** every day.

4. _____ Doing your homework in a quiet place is a good **plan**.

5. _____ I use my new **phone** all the time.

6. _____ In the morning, I **water** my plants.

Prefixes *in-* and *im-*

Remember: A prefix is a small group of letters that come at the beginning of a word. Like *un-*, the prefixes *in-* and *im-* mean "not." You can add them to the beginning of some adjectives to make a word with the opposite meaning. Look in a dictionary to check for the correct spelling.

in + *expensive* = *inexpensive*, or "not expensive."

A Write *un-*, *im-*, or *in-* before each adjective. Use a dictionary to help you.

1. Some social media posts have _____ correct information.

2. I didn't like that movie. It was really _____ interesting.

3. Sometimes a movie review can be really _____ helpful.

4. It's _____ polite to talk during a movie.

5. The movie was over four hours long! It was _____ possible to watch it all.

Word forms Adjectives with *-ed* and *-ing* endings

We can use adjectives that end in *-ed* and *-ing* to describe feelings, but we use them differently.

Adjectives with *-ed* usually refer to something someone feels.
Adjectives with *-ing* usually refer to something that causes a feeling.

*I was **bored**.* = Something makes me feel this way.
*The movie was **boring**.* = The movie causes the feeling.

B Choose the correct adjective form to complete each sentence.

A: Did you like the movie?

B. Yes, I thought it was **interested / interesting**. The special effects were **amazed / amazing**.

A. I agree. I was **surprised / surprising** about the ending.

B. Really? It **confused / confusing** me.

A. Yeah, it was **confused / confusing**.

B. Let's go home. I'm **tired / tiring**.

Suffix -ly

Remember: A suffix is a small group of letters that come at the end of a word. You can add -ly to the end of some adjectives to change them to adverbs. If an adjective ends in -y, change the -y to an -i.

We can use adverbs before an adjective or verb.

ADJECTIVE	ADVERB	EXAMPLE
actual	actual**ly**	I **actually** like to try new things.
easy	eas**ily**	I am **easily** bored.

A Complete the paragraph with the adjective or adverb form of the words in parentheses.

My name is Kim. I'm studying photography at school. I'm ¹_____ (near) finished

with my classes. I like taking pictures of people. I am creative and hard-working. I'm

²_____ (actual) top of my class! I'm ³_____ (real) not sure what job I

want. I could be a photographer. But photography is not an ⁴_____ (easy) profession to

get into. I am ⁵_____ (willing) to work for a local newspaper or magazine. I'll need to

think ⁶_____ (careful) about my plans.

Using context Restatement

When we learn a new word or phrase, it is helpful to restate it. This means we say the same thing in a different or easier way. This helps us to remember the meaning of the word or phrase. A vocabulary journal is a good place to do this.

PHRASE   RESTATEMENT
I'm **doing well** in my biology class. I **got an "A"** on the test!

PHRASE   RESTATEMENT
I **hardly ever** talk with my manager, or **not often**.

B Underline the words or phrases that restate the words in bold.

1. I am **talented** at math. I'm especially good at it.

2. I prefer to **work remotely,** or work from home.

3. I **failed** the test. I did very badly.

4. I want to be a **pediatrician**, or kid's doctor, after college.

5. I want to **get into** a good college. I hope one will accept me!

Using a dictionary Synonyms

Synonyms are words that are similar in meaning. The words *large* and *big* are synonyms. A dictionary may include synonyms in a box labeled *Thesaurus* or marked with the abbreviation *SYN*. You can also look for synonyms in a thesaurus.

THESAURUS
trash (n) garbage, junk, rubbish, litter

A Use a dictionary. Match each word with the correct synonym.

1. _____ young (adj)   a. fix

2. _____ amazing (adj)   b. childish

3. _____ several (adj)   c. anxious

4. _____ repair (v)   d. tiny

5. _____ worried (adj)   e. quite a few

6. _____ small (adj)   f. surprising

B Write two sentences using two of the synonyms above.

1. _____

2. _____

Homophones

Homophones are words that sound the same but have different spellings and meanings. For example, *meat* and *meet* are pronounced the same but *meat* refers to food and *meet* means *to join someone at a given location.*

When you are listening to someone speak, use context to understand which meaning is correct. When you are reading, both the context and the spelling can help you.

C Choose the best word to complete each sentence. Use a dictionary to help you.

1. The Environment Club **meets / meats** every Saturday in the library.

2. The **son / sun** is not causing global warming.

3. I got a letter in the **male / mail** about global warming.

4. The **sea / see** is getting higher because of global warming.

5. Taking care of the environment is the **right / write** thing to do.

VOCABULARY INDEX

Unit 1	Page	CEFR
agree	10	A2
be called	4	A1
be interested in	4	A2
believe	10	A2
far	10	A2
fast	10	A1
free time	4	A2
friendly	4	A2
goal*	10	B1
hard	10	A1
idea	4	B1
job*	4	A1
last	10	A2
matter	10	A2
meet	4	A1
size	10	A2
smile	4	B1
thin	10	A2
way	4	A2
wrong	4	A1

Unit 2	Page	CEFR
alone	20	A2
chat	26	A2
comfortable	20	A2
cozy	26	B1
during	20	A2
holiday	26	A1
home	20	A1
memory	26	B1
move	20	A2
(one's) own	20	B1
place	26	A1
present	26	B1
really	26	A1
relax*	26	B1
share	20	A2
smell	26	B1
space	20	A2
sunny	20	A2
there	20	A1
trust	26	B1

Unit 3	Page	CEFR
check	36	A2
daily	36	A2
diary*	42	A2
every	36	A1
exercise	42	A2
feel	42	A1
get	36	A1
habit	42	B1
instead	42	A2
kind	36	A1
moment	42	B1
more	42	A1
part	36	A1
show	36	A1
too	42	A1
track	42	C2
travel	36	A1
try	42	A2
visit	36	A1
water	36	A1

Unit 4	Page	CEFR
bring	52	A2
connect	52	B1
delicious	52	B1
dessert	52	A2
healthy	58	A2
hungry	52	A1
maybe	58	A2
meal	52	A1
normal*	58	A2
recipe*	52	B1
restaurant	52	A1
sad	58	A1
salty	58	B2
sick	52	A2
snack	58	A2
special	52	A1
spicy	58	B1
stressed*	58	B1
sweet	58	A1
tired	58	A1

*Academic Words

VOCABULARY INDEX

IRREGULAR VERB FORMS

Base form	Simple past	Past participle
be	was, were	been
beat	beat	beaten
become	became	become
begin	began	begun
bend	bent	bent
bite	bit	bitten
blow	blew	blown
break	broke	broken
bring	brought	brought
build	built	built
buy	bought	bought
catch	caught	caught
choose	chose	chosen
come	came	come
cost	cost	cost
cut	cut	cut
dig	dug	dug
dive	dived/dove	dived
do	did	done
draw	drew	drawn
drink	drank	drunk
drive	drove	driven
eat	ate	eaten
fall	fell	fallen
feed	fed	fed
feel	felt	felt
fight	fought	fought
find	found	found
fit	fit	fit/fitted
fly	flew	flown
forget	forgot	forgotten
forgive	forgave	forgiven
freeze	froze	frozen
get	got	got/gotten
give	gave	given
go	went	gone
grow	grew	grown
hang	hung	hung
have	had	had
hear	heard	heard
hide	hid	hidden
hit	hit	hit
hold	held	held
hurt	hurt	hurt
keep	kept	kept
know	knew	known

Base form	Simple past	Past participle
lay	laid	laid
lead	led	led
leave	left	left
lend	lent	lent
let	let	let
lie	lay	lain
light	lit/lighted	lit/lighted
lose	lost	lost
make	made	made
mean	meant	meant
meet	met	met
pay	paid	paid
prove	proved	proved/proven
put	put	put
quit	quit	quit
read	read	read
ride	rode	ridden
ring	rang	rung
rise	rose	risen
run	ran	run
say	said	said
sit	sat	sat
sleep	slept	slept
slide	slid	slid
speak	spoke	spoken
spend	spent	spent
spread	spread	spread
stand	stood	stood
steal	stole	stolen
stick	stuck	stuck
strike	struck	struck
swear	swore	sworn
sweep	swept	swept
swim	swam	swum
take	took	taken
teach	taught	taught
tear	tore	torn
tell	told	told
think	thought	thought
throw	threw	thrown
understand	understood	understood
upset	upset	upset
wake	woke	woken
wear	wore	worn
win	won	won
write	wrote	written

SOUNDS & SYMBOLS

Vowel sounds

1. **e**at, sl**ee**p /iʸ/
2. **i**t, s**i**p /ɪ/
3. l**a**te, r**ai**n /eʸ/
4. w**e**t, p**e**n /ɛ/
5. c**a**t, f**a**n /æ/
6. b**i**rd, t**u**rn /ɜr/
7. c**u**t, s**u**n /ʌ/
   about, b**e**fore /ə/ (schwa)
8. n**o**t, t**o**p /ɑ/
9. t**oo**, f**ew** /uʷ/
10. g**oo**d, sh**ou**ld /ʊ/
11. t**oe**, n**o** /oʷ/
12. s**aw**, w**a**lk /ɔ/

Dipthongs

13. f**i**ne, r**i**ce /ay/
14. **ou**t, n**ow** /aw/
15. b**oy**, j**oin** /ɔy/

Consonant sounds

1. **p**en /p/
2. **b**ag /b/
3. **t**ime /t/
4. **d**og /d/
5. **k**eep /k/
6. **g**et /g/
7. **f**eel /f/
8. **v**ery /v/
9. **th**in /θ/
10. **th**e /ð/
11. **s**ale /s/
12. ea**s**y, cau**s**e /z/
13. **sh**e /ʃ/
14. trea**s**ure /ʒ/
15. **ch**icken /tʃ/
16. **j**oin /dʒ/
17. **m**e /m/
18. **n**ot /n/
19. ri**ng** /ŋ/
20. **l**ose /l/
21. **r**ead, **wr**ite /r/
22. **w**in /w/
23. **y**ou /y/
24. **h**ome /h/

COMMON TERMS

syllables: a unit of sound; one or more syllables make a word. A syllable in English has one vowel sound and 1-3 consonant sounds at the beginning or end.

book, re-flect, a-ca-de-mic

word stress: the syllable in a word that is said more loudly and strongly

*book, re-**flect**, a-ca-**de**-mic*

sentence stress: the words in a sentence that are said more loudly and strongly, usually content words (nouns, verbs, adjectives, adverbs)

*I **stu**dy aca**de**mic **En**glish with Re**flect**.*

focus word: the most important word in a phrase or sentence; it usually provides new information and has the most stress. It is often the last word in a phrase or sentence.

*I study **En**glish. I use a book called Re**flect**.*

intonation: the rise and fall of the voice (or pitch). Often our voice falls at the end of a sentence.

*I **stu**dy aca**de**mic **En**glish with Re**flect**.*

USEFUL PHRASES FOR CLASSROOM COMMUNICATION

EXPRESS YOURSELF

Express opinions

think...   *In my opinion/view...*
I believe...   *Personally,...*
I'm (not) sure... *To me,...*

Express likes and dislikes

I like...   *I hate...*
I prefer... *I really don't like...*
I love...   *don't care for...*

Give facts

Studies show...
Researchers found...
The record shows...

Give tips or suggestions

You/We should/shouldn't/could...
You/We ought to...   It's (not) a good idea to...
Let's...   Why don't we/you...

Agree with someone

I agree. Absolutely.
True. Definitely
Good point. Right!
Exactly.

Disagree with someone

I disagree.
I'm not so sure about that.
I don't know.
That's a good point, but I don't agree.

PARTICIPATE IN CLASSROOM DISCUSSIONS

Check your understanding

So are you saying that...?
So what you mean is...?
What do you mean?
Do you mean...?
I'm not sure what you mean.

Ask for repetition

Could you say that again?
I'm sorry?
I didn't catch what you said.
I'm sorry. I missed that. What did you say?
Could you repeat that please?

Check others' understanding

Does that make sense?
Do you understand?
Is that clear?
Do you have any questions?

Ask for opinions

What do you think?
Do you have any thoughts?
What are your thoughts?
What's your opinion?

Take turns

Can/May I say something?
Could I add something?
Your turn.
You go ahead.

Interrupt politely

Excuse me.
Pardon me.
Forgive me for interrupting, but...
I hate to interrupt, but...

Make small talk

What do you do? (job)
Can you believe this weather?
How about this weather?
What do you do in your free time?
What do you do for fun?

Show interest

I see. Good for you.
Really? Seriously?
Um-hmm. No kidding!
Wow. And? (Then what?)
That's funny / amazing / incredible / awful!

INDEX OF EXAM SKILLS & TASKS

Reflect is designed to provide practice for standardized exams, such as IELTS and TOEFL. This book has many activities that focus on and practice skills and question types that are needed for test success.

CREDITS